ELIZABETH BREWSTER

The Invention of Truth

Acknowledgements: "Victorian Interlude" was first published in *Event.* "Visit of Condolence" originally appeared in *Western Living* and *Sky High.* "Collage" was originally published in *Visitations* and "Essence of Marigold" first appeared in *A House Full of Women.*

ISBN 0 88750 869 3 (hardcover)
ISBN 0 88750 870 7 (softcover)

Cover art by Chery Holmes
Book design by Michael Macklem

Printed in Canada

PUBLISHED IN CANADA BY OBERON PRESS

The Invention of Truth: Beginnings

One friend of mine tells me that I have been writing autobiography all my life. In some senses this is true, but then what is autobiography? Is everything any author writes autobiographical, since (even if she wishes) she cannot go totally beyond the boundaries of her experience and observation? Emily Brontë may never have met anyone resembling Heathcliff but at least she knew him as the projection of her own desires and fears. Shakespeare may never have been tempted to smother his wife or yearned to become a king but he was an unusual human being if he never—even perhaps as a very young child—experienced jealousy, envy, the longing for power. "Know thyself," "Dig within," the old sages said. Is that "digging in" unhealthily narcissistic, or is it one of the ways of knowing the other? What are the bounds between the self and the other? And what is the self anyway?

I think everything I have ever written has been an attempt to approach truth, at least a personal truth. Some truth is factual, some is fictional, some is poetic. Fact, fiction and poetry are all, in a way, made up—confections, to use a more frivolous (though related) word. To write any of the three involves invention (a coming upon) or discovery (an act of uncovering). The discovery or invention of truth is not easy. It requires as many approaches as possible, and none of them will ever be completely successful.

I began writing diaries, fiction and poetry at more or less the same time, when I was a child of nine or ten. I had read a novel in diary form, a "dear diary" novel, and thought I should keep a diary too. But nothing happened. What was I to do? I filled out the entries with poems. I wrote a long, rambling fiction, a fantasy about two children, a boy and a girl, who wandered away from home into an enchanted forest, where they encountered a princess who lived in a castle and sang to the accompaniment of a harp. (Not much fact there, but perhaps some truth: the adventure I wanted to have, the beauty I wanted to encounter or create.) I could not imagine what song the princess sang. I asked my elder sister to write one for me, but she wrote instead a song for fairies dancing in a round. I had to write the princess's song myself, and invent another episode in which the children saw the fairies dancing.

Adolescence let loose a flood of poems, derivative and sentimental, I'm afraid. I remember a long narrative poem in Spenserian stanzas, imitative of Sir Walter Scott. It was set in Ireland (which of course I had never seen) and was titled "Aileen," but I have no further recollection of it. There were poems on the seasons, chiefly autumn. (One of these was my first published poem, published in the Saint John *Telegraph* when I was twelve.) I was religious and tried to write hymns. I have no doubt they were sincere, but I'm thankful I did not save them. Yet I wrote these early poems with as much seriousness, with perhaps more passion, more ambition, than I ever wrote anything later. I felt more often that excitement, that sense of being taken over, that one calls "inspiration." (L.M. Montgomery's Emily called it "the flash," but I hadn't read the Emily books then.) Is such inspiration then a pure delusion, since the results could be so mediocre? Maybe not. Maybe there were genuine insights, but I had not the language to express them.

I look this over, and decide that I am going in too straight a line, organizing my thoughts too firmly. What am I trying to do? To narrate the growth of a poet's mind, in my particular time and place? Is it arrogant of me to set out to do what Wordsworth was doing in the *Prelude?* But Wordsworth was a rather unfashionable poet when he wrote the *Prelude.* Anyhow, I'm not choosing Wordsworth's order, am I?

I read that diary novel when I was seven years old, visiting my Grandmother Day, my mother's mother. On my seventh birthday (in August, 1929) my grandmother said to me, "You're one-tenth of my age, exactly," for she was 70. And that evening I sat on the back steps, and thought how old I was, and how many years it would be before I reached Grandma's age, and all the things I might write in my diary in the next 60 or so years. My two younger cousins, Pauline and Marie, sat on the back steps with me, and I read aloud to them from the novel. I never stumbled on that novel again. It was full of emotion, of someone seeing herself as full of faults. "Is it all true?" I asked my mother. "No," she said, "it's a novel."

On Sunday afternoons, when we were visiting Grandma, my mother used to read sentimental novels, lying on the bed with me beside her. I wasn't supposed to make a noise on Sunday; reading along with Mother kept me quiet. That was the room where I was born, she told me. I used to feel a shiver of strangeness when people said, "That happened before you were born." I would shut my eyes and try to remember back and back in time. I would remember some early things—the Christmas I was three, when I got blocks with letters on them; a rag doll my mother sewed for me—but at some point I would encounter blackness. I couldn't remember before I was born. I couldn't even remember a time when I couldn't read.

It was that same year (the year of my seventh birthday) that I read *The Scarlet Letter,* for the sake of little Pearl, and the brook, and the forest, and the witches. And I read Hans Andersen's fairytales, and before that some of Grimm, and poems from Mother Goose. The lovely jangle of rhyme. The first serious, ambitious poem I remember reading was Shelley's cloud poem, or an excerpt from it in some publication, the summer I was eight. I cut it out and put it in a scrapbook I was keeping. I saved poems I cut from magazines, as I saved the pennies I was given in a little metal bank that had held jelly beans for Christmas. Just after my eighth birthday a young man came to the door of the farmhouse we were renting for the summer. He was selling Bibles, and I dumped out all my pennies on the kitchen table so that I could buy a New Testament. I started reading at the end, and encountered the beautiful, frightening poetry of the Book of Revelations. I had read Bible stories before, in a book of Bible stories with the alphabet in front; and I had heard my mother read from the Bible in the evening, when I was sitting on her knee. But I had never encountered anything like this. "I am Alpha and Omega, the beginning and the end." What were Alpha and Omega? It didn't matter; the words were beautiful. And how marvellous that picture of the New Jerusalem, an enchanted city descending from the sky.

It's not surprising, maybe, that by the time I was twelve I had read my way through the whole Bible, except for the Apocrypha, which wasn't in my mother's Bible. Some of it was a great task and trial; but I loved Job, and Jonah, and Ruth, and the Psalms, and the Song of Songs, and some of the New Testament. I also read most of Shakespeare. My father had given my mother a Collected Shakespeare (with rather poor illustrations) for one of her birthdays. I began with *A Midsummer Night's Dream* and *The Tempest*. Perhaps that's the reason my tale of the children lost in the woods had to include songs.

Someone reading this now might think I'm trying to show off how precocious I was as a child. But I read what was lying around, which also included funny papers (Little Orphan Annie, Our Boarding House, Tillie the Toiler), Sunday School papers, the *Family Herald and Weekly Star* which included serialized versions of novels by Agatha Christie and P.G. Wodehouse.

From the time I was eight to the time I was twelve, we lived on a rundown, unprosperous farm on the Washademoak Lake, in Queen's County, New Brunswick. My sister Eleanor and I attended the one-room school at Hammtown. Eleanor, who was four years older than I, left the school at fourteen, and I attended the two final years by myself. The Washademoak was certainly not a rural paradise, though I have some fond memories of it. I used the Washademoak, under the name of Moss Lake, as the setting for much of my novel *The Sisters*. It was one of the most beautiful places I have ever seen; but we were so poor that we were always on the verge of starvation. (I remember that the sandwiches I took to school for lunch were usually bread and jam.) Perhaps also I didn't always fit in well with the other students, though I don't remember troubles the first year or so, not until Eleanor left school. Then I was the runt of the school, not the youngest but the smallest. Children, of course, are natural bullies. For months the two Corcoran girls, Eileen and Blanche, used to beat me up on the way home from school. Did they have any reason? I can't think of any, except that I was weak and weakness invites bullying. I didn't tell any of the grownups, teachers or parents. I knew that tattling was the greatest of all sins. However, they finally went too far. They took me down and removed the little gold ring with my initials that my sister Marion had given me for my birthday, bought with money from helping at housework in Saint John. Marion, when she found the ring was missing, wanted to know how I could be so careless as to lose it. Of course I had to tell her the truth, and she rushed off in full fury to confront the girls. After supper they came to the door and handed the ring to my mother. Curiously, after that the Corcoran girls and I became rather friendly. When I left the Washademoak, we pledged eternal friendship, or at least promised to write—if we could afford the postage.

My sister Marion said to me years afterwards, "They broke your spirit." Not broke, I think. Bent.

Perhaps I came to feel that books—or pencil and paper—were more dependable friends than other girls and boys were. Certainly I spent much time, then and later, by myself. Sometimes I was bored; but boredom is a great inducement to reading and writing. And sometimes I was perfectly, blissfully happy. I used to take books in summer to the crook of an old tree overlooking the Lake. Other times I wrote in the little bedroom up the back stairs from the kitchen.

At first I didn't show what I wrote to anyone; but I came home from school one afternoon and found one of my sisters reading aloud to my mother from the story I was writing. I was much injured; it seemed to me an intrusion and a betrayal. I ran up the back stairs to bury myself away from them; but they called me down, and told me they liked the story, and asked me to read it aloud to them. I think of that incident whenever anyone asks me, "And what audience do you write for?" (First, of course, for oneself; then for anyone who snoops or overhears.)

I tried to write stories, plays, poems, even a little newspaper—though of course there was no news. Later, I attempted sermons. Sometimes I thought I would like to be a missionary when I grew up; sometimes, a journalist.

In 1934, when I was twelve, we left the Washademoak, and spent the next four years in or near Chipman. Chipman I've also written about in *The Sisters* and to some extent in my long narrative poem *Lillooet,* my short story "Visiting Aunt Alix," and some of my poems, such as those about my Great-Aunt Rebecca.

This was the most painful period of my growing up, and probably the most painful period for my parents, too. It was harsh enough as I narrated it in *The Sisters* but harsher still as we lived through it.

We lived for the first year or so in an old dilapidated house outside of town, called the Pest House because a group of people had been quarantined there in the distant past with some disease. It was a long distance to school; I didn't have good shoes or overshoes; somehow I dropped out of school for three years. If I had been ambitious, no doubt I would have found a way to go, but I didn't. Of course I went on reading. I remember sitting with my feet in the oven of the old wood stove to keep them warm, while I read *A Tale of Two Cities* and *Great Expectations* and *Oliver Twist.* My father tried to make a little money selling magazine subscriptions. My mother helped a number of housewives with their spring-cleaning, or her nieces with the birth of their babies. I went along on these excursions, helped out with a little dishwashing, read any books on the premises. Sometimes the pickings were slim: Cousin Myrtle had only the Bible, the Collected Poems of Tennyson and Eaton's catalogue. Cousin Remona had the Books of Knowledge, which I brought out one by one from the frigid, unheated living-room where they were kept. But Isaac Baird's family had a whole array of books: that was where I first read *Pride and Prejudice* and *Jane Eyre* and Boswell's *Life of Johnson* and *Journal to the Hebrides.* Frank Baird (was he Isaac's brother or uncle?) had been Moderator of the Presbyterian

Church and the author of historical novels. One of Isaac's sisters had married the President of the University of New Brunswick. The idea of university first entered my mind then, especially when a Baird grandson with a scholarship visited. I told my mother that I would like to go back to school, though by this time I was fifteen. So we moved into town—on the wrong side of the tracks, of course, but town, all the same—in what was nicknamed Rabbit Town.

I wonder now what kind of a writer I would have been if I had not gone back to school. Sarah Binks or Alden Nowlan? Certainly Alden managed to give himself a good education without benefit of school or university. I might have done so too. There was not much mental stimulation in elementary school, certainly. I was simply carried along by my desire to escape the trap of poverty, the life of "bread-and-perhaps," as Alden called it. (Perhaps there would be molasses with the bread, perhaps not.)

Writing was something separate from school. It involved ambition, maybe, but a different kind of ambition, and anyway was largely something to enjoy. It was my father who sent off that poem of mine to the Saint John *Telegraph,* when I was twelve, and I had a few more published there. When I was fourteen, I sent off a group of poems to one of the few New Brunswick writers whose names I knew, H.A. Cody. Cody, who was an Archdeacon in St. James' Church in Saint John, was the author of poems and historical novels (among them *The King's Arrow,* which I had read because it was set in the neighbourhood of the Washademoak Lake). He wrote me a kind and sensible letter telling me that my poems had promise, encouraging me to go on writing, but warning me that I must not expect to make a living out of them. "Bliss Carman," he wrote, "was always so poor, and yet he was so very well known." I may have had some childish daydreams of becoming rich and famous through my writing. I put away the dream of riches. I would earn my living in some other way. But did I need to put away the dream of fame? Might I at least have my poems in the school readers like poor Bliss Carman? Perhaps that letter was one of the reasons for my going back to school.

My parents and I moved to Sussex in the summer of 1938. It was a purely chance move and might have been as miserable as some of the others; but fortunately it was not. Sussex also occurs as a background in *The Sisters,* as the town of Milton. A pleasant, idyllic rural small town, it was somewhat changed in 1939, when war revitalized the army camp that had been there in the first Great War. In the Sussex School I was lucky enough to have several good teachers, especially Nane Mac-Neill and Ethel Singer. Miss MacNeill lent me books of poetry and books about poetry and, eventually, was the person most responsible for persuading me to apply for a scholarship to university. I was helped also by my friend and rival, Phyllis King, who was in my class in school. Phyllis and I were both omnivorous readers, reading books aloud to each other. We borrowed books from the small village library (upstairs over the fire station) and my father also brought me home books from the Army Camp, where he worked in the Army Canteen. It was Phyllis who suggested that we both send poems and stories to a contest run regularly by the United Church Sunday School paper. She tended to win for prose, I for poetry, though sometimes for prose as well. The judges definitely preferred metre to free verse; a sonnet or a villanelle was sure to get some kind of credit, at least for the attempt. Miriam Waddington told me years later that she had also had a number of poems published on that page, I suppose a few years earlier. Probably this encouragement to school-age writers came about because the publisher of the Sunday School paper was also the publisher of Ryerson Press books. The judge did discourage clichés, I think, and preferred a certain solidity in the material. Burbling was not encouraged. Not a bad influence, on the whole.

One person I met during this high-school period was P.K.

Page. I sent some poems to a contest of the New Brunswick Authors Association in Saint John. Pat, a young poet herself, was one of the judges. She wrote to me, and a visit to Saint John was arranged. I used this visit, very much changed, as the basis of my short story "Essence of Marigold" (in *A House Full of Women*). I have to admit that I did not win a prize on this occasion—only an honourable mention—though Pat had clear memories of my winning one. But memory is shifting and changeable. I was much younger than the man who won the prize; perhaps the judges thought at the time that I had the promise, he had the accomplishment.

I was certainly very much impressed with Pat herself as a person and a writer. She sent me a few of her poems, and wrote me about the novel she was working on, I suppose the one published later under the title *The Sun and the Moon*. By the time it was published she had grown away from it and so published it under a pseudonym; but, though I can see why she may have reacted against it (the mix of realistic social detail with fairytale and symbol doesn't always work) it seems to me to be a powerful and mysterious fiction.

I came back from that Saint John visit in a state of ecstatic enthusiasm about Pat and about the meeting of authors I had attended. I'm afraid I may have burbled a bit. Probably I amused Phyllis and Miss MacNeill and Miss Singer, who were always there. I seem to have some recollection of Miss Singer smiling and teasing me a bit about this brilliant, remarkable young woman who was spending her time typing away at her novel of a young woman and an artist. Was this a substantial background for a novel? What would I write a novel about myself?

I think I was right to think that Pat was remarkable. The fact that she was there, she was writing, she took my poems seriously, meant a lot to me then and later. Nane MacNeill and Ethel Singer also meant much to me. They helped me with all those dull mechanics of reading and writing. They made sure I—and many of the students in their classes—would pass matriculation creditably when we came to write exams. I never thanked them before I graduated—I might've thought they would think I was apple polishing. Later, after I went away to university, I forgot about it.

And university was a different world.

University Days: Dreamer and Dream

"I was the Dreamer, they the Dream," so Wordsworth wrote of himself and his surroundings in his college days at Cambridge, at least on his first arrival. Do university students now have this feeling of strangeness, of entering a new world where they hardly recognize themselves? Certainly I wondered at times if I were dreaming in those early days at the University of New Brunswick. My parents had not gone to university, nor had any of my brothers and sisters. A few years ago I had even dropped out of school. When I went back to school, I thought I might some time manage university, but not directly after graduation from high school. However, here I was in Fredericton in September, 1942, about to start university. I had a small entrance scholarship, enough to pay for tuition and books. My parents had moved to Fredericton that summer. My father worked as a night watchman at the army canteen; my mother made doughnuts for the canteen, as she had in Sussex. They could provide me with room and meals; they could not have afforded to send me away from home to board. I don't suppose my father would have had a job at all if it had not been for the War. (Perhaps one reason why there were no peace marches in those days was that there were many people in similar circumstances.)

We lived within walking distance of the university, in the downstairs of a small house on Needham Street. There was a rambling, old-fashioned flower garden in front, and space at the rear for a vegetable garden. The house itself was rather down-at-heel and unpainted. There was no furnace; the rooms were heated in the winter by the wood stove in the kitchen and a second wood heater in the combined dining- and-living-room. The only running water was in the kitchen. There was a toilet off the kitchen; we took our baths in a round metal tub that hung on the wall and was brought down for each bath. The bedroom off the dining-room was tiny but warm. The front bedroom (usually mine) was larger but frigid. In a really cold January, the more comfortable spot was the sofa in the dining-room, in between two fires. All this sounds rather grim; yet I remember the house as attractive in its unpretending way, when my mother had scrubbed it from top to bottom and put fresh curtains at the windows and her own hooked rugs on the floor. There were bookcases that my father had made and painted; there was a comfortable chair with a faded red cover; there was a rather pretty little desk that my parents gave me for Christmas. I liked the house, especially in the warmer seasons of the year; and even in cold weather the central rooms were cheerful. Sometimes we were startled by noises from upstairs. A young truck driver and his wife lived in the upstairs flat; they were given to loud quarrels and intense reconciliations. Later, the husband joined the Army, and the wife was left by herself for a time with her baby daughter. She and I had the same first name and were close to each other in age; but somehow we were shy of one another. It was with my mother that she became friendly.

Fredericton at this time was a small, green, peaceful city of around eight thousand people. It would hardly have been called a city if it had not contained a cathedral, the provincial university and the provincial government buildings. Like Sussex, it had a military camp, but it was a smaller camp, and did not seem to dominate the town as the one at Sussex had. Perhaps the War in fact made the city seem more peaceful than in other circumstances. Rationing of gasoline and tires made motor traffic light. People drove cars only when absolutely necessary. At the university, faculty and students walked or rode bicycles. I don't remember any motorcycles, at least none that anybody drove for fun. Liquor rationing probably prevented loud parties. Now and then a military band played marches on the Green on a Sunday afternoon, but it was long before the time of rock concerts or any really loud music. Soldiers strolled on Queen Street on shopping nights, and sometimes there were sailors in town on a course, but they saved most of their quarrels for other times and places.

The university, like the city, was small. A sociable person could have known all the faculty and students. Even a comparatively unsociable person like me knew many. There was a mere handful of buildings clustered on top of the only hill in town, with a view of the river and the church spires and the trees below, red and gold in the warm light of the autumn in which I first saw them. Most of my classes were in the Arts Building, a handsome old Georgian structure, and I divided my time between it and the library—small by the standards of great universities, but large for one who had gone to school in Hammtown, Chipman and Sussex.

I don't suppose going to university in war time was much different from going at other times. Classes were smaller, especially senior classes. Some of the young men who came to university in my first year had signed up for one of the Armed Services by the second or third year. In my final year, of course, the War was over, and the young men came back—some of them, or others in their place—and the university was crowded. The summer of 1942 was a worrying time in the War—the summer of Dieppe—with long lists of casualties, but I had not yet had any friend or relative killed or wounded. No doubt the fact of the War hovered in the back of my mind, but I was too busy with this new experience of university to allow myself to think much about it. Perhaps I willed myself not to think of it. There was not yet television. Now and then I saw a war film, but I suspected such films to be censored, and no doubt they were. We did not own a radio. There was, of course, the daily paper; but this war had gone on too long. I read the headlines. Cousins and cousins-in-law came through town, in one uniform or another. I heard some of the rumours, about secret weapons on the enemy's side or ours. My sister Marion's lover was in the Army. So was my second brother, who hated it. The elder of my brothers, who would dearly have loved to sign up, was stone deaf and couldn't. Did I think I ought to have joined the CWACs? No, I think not. I was better suited to life at university, reading Milton and Virgil and Plato, writing poems in my spare time.

There were no courses in Creative Writing in the university at that time; but Edward McCourt, who taught my English courses the first two years, was a fiction writer who later produced a series of prairie novels, among them *Music at the Close, Home is the Stranger* and *The Wooden Sword.* I showed my poems to him, as well as to Professor Smethurst, who taught Latin and Greek. It was McCourt who typed out a group of poems for me so that I could enter a university competition for a prize, which I won. In my second year I joined the small poetry society—limited to seven students—that met in A.G. Bailey's living-room. Bailey, an anthropologist and historian, was an accomplished, erudite poet. I never took a course from him; but it was at his suggestion that I read Toynbee, Spengler, Proust, the novels and poems of Robert Graves, and Frazer's *Golden Bough.* Bailey was a T.S. Eliot enthusiast, and my first acquaintance with Eliot's poetry came, not in the English classroom (McCourt preferred poetry from earlier in the century; I think his favourite was Thomas Hardy) but in the Baileys' living-room, where Bailey recited parts of *The Waste Land,* as well as fragments from the *Four Quartets,* just coming out. He was interested in current Canadian poetry too. He knew Earle Birney, and read us sections of *David,* a recent poem then. He subscribed to *Preview,* the small mimeographed magazine coming out of Montreal. I subscribed to it myself, when I saw that it included poems by Pat Page, though I had lost touch with her when she left Saint John and I left Sussex. Of course, it also included poems by Frank Scott and A.M. Klein and Patrick Anderson, who was something of a cult figure at the time. One of our little Group of Seven, Jack Jeans, a flamboyant young man with red hair, used to recite Anderson's "Summer's Joe," standing in the main lobby of the Arts Building and leaning against a pillar.

Our group was officially named the Bliss Carman Society, though we were rather uncomfortable with the name. No doubt Carman was an old-fashioned poet, but he and Charles Roberts were part of our local tradition. In fact, I had a sneaking fondness for Roberts' sonnets about burnt lands and cow pastures and potato fields: they told of a landscape I knew almost too well. And some of Carman's lines still remain with me:

> The windows of my room
> Are dark with bitter frost.

I knew what that meant, as I tried to find a peephole in the window-panes of the cold front bedroom. I could not, like

Wordsworth, sit in the room where Milton once slept, or see the marble head of Newton and think of that mighty mind "voyaging through strange seas of Thought, alone." But I glimpsed Charles Roberts when he visited St. Anne's Church, where his father had once been the pastor, and I walked past the house where Carman had lived. Thede Roberts, Charles' younger brother, came to read to our English class—a charmer, though an elderly charmer.

Of the seven of us in the Bliss Carman Society at the time I joined, I am the only one who went on writing; but some of the others were talented. I don't know what happened to our flamboyant Jack Jeans. Someone told me he died young, but not how he died. Don Gammon, the first editor of our little mimeographed magazine, *The Fiddlehead,* was my classmate and close friend. Frances Firth, whom he later married, was one of my closest friends in the group. So was Eleanor Belyea. Don, Frances and Eleanor are all still my friends. The one I chiefly admired was Norwood Carter, a brilliant, handsome, remote (perhaps shy) young man. I was intimidated by him and imagined I loved him. He was not only in my English class but (along with Jack Jeans) in the classes I took in Latin and Greek, which included only a handful of students. I admired him so much that I could not quite believe it when Professor Smethurst told me he was overshadowed by his elder brother Erskine, who had also been academically brilliant and who was now in one of the armed services. Was it Erskine who kept himself intellectually alive during the time he was a POW by reading the small copy of Virgil he had in his pocket? I would have liked to think Norwood's poetry was better than mine, but in fact I knew it wasn't. His poems were, as I remember them, thoughtful and technically accomplished, but lacking in the final spark of energy or enthusiasm. If he had gone on writing perhaps some fire would have descended, but so far as I know he did not write poems after he left university to join the Navy. That was, I think, at Christmas, in the middle of our second year. I never saw him again.

When he came back after the War, he went to McGill rather than to UNB, graduated from the McGill Law School, and—like his brother Erskine—was a Rhodes Scholar at Oxford. It must have been about Norwood that I wrote back then, sentimentally, "Stars, moons, and suns shine in your eyes/And where you are is Paradise." My mother sent me the notice of his wedding (by then I was in Graduate School). Someone told me that the War had been hard on him. Someone else said he was not as successful as his academic brilliance might have led one to expect, that he had some reasons for unhappiness and disappointment. He died suddenly, in early middle age. I read the death notice in a newspaper on a plane flying from Fredericton to Toronto. If his funeral had not been private, with only the family present, I might have stopped in Toronto to go to it.

I can't remember who was the seventh student in that poetry group. A senior student, I think, who also went into the Services. Desmond Pacey arrived in time to help, as faculty adviser with A.G. Bailey, with that first issue of the *Fiddlehead.* Later Margaret Cunningham came to the group, and, in my final year, after the War was over, Fred Cogswell, who for many years edited the *Fiddlehead* and later the Fiddlehead Poetry Books, and who became well known as a poet and a translator.

I had, of course, friends who did not try to write poetry. I belonged to the Dramatic Society; wrote a regular column for the student newspaper, the *Brunswickan;* worked part-time for the university library. I had, as I recall it, a number of warm friendships, but, sadly, no lovers, though I yearned for one. I blamed my plain face, my shabby clothing, my shyness (which sometimes looked like arrogance), my inability to talk casually on frivolous subjects. I'm told I seemed chilly. One of my friends said that Norwood would have been interested in me if I had shown I was interested in him, but how could I have shown interest?

In the summer of 1944, Edward McCourt left for the University of Saskatchewan. He had been our total English Department, and was replaced by Desmond Pacey. I was depressed by McCourt's departure. I had been working on the draft of a novel, which he had read sympathetically. His departure, after Norwood's and along with that of several other student friends, seemed to leave a sense of emptiness. That was the summer of D-Day, the Normandy invasion, the crisis of the European part of the War, after which victory, though unbearably delayed, seemed surely inevitable. But casualties were also inevitable. One of my cousins was listed as missing, presumed dead. His younger brother was already a prisoner of war. Was it around this time that I wrote a rather bad anti-war sonnet, bitterly complaining of the "fools and hypocrites" who were fighting "an equal band of hypocrites and fools"? The next year a favourite aunt, my mother's youngest sister, Grace, died unexpectedly, not much more than 40. It's not surprising that many of my poems of the time were much concerned with death. A few of these I liked well enough to keep for publication much later, in my *Selected Poems*.

I was sometimes profoundly unhappy in this period, and could only get to sleep at night by repeating to myself in my mind, "Nothing matters, nothing matters." I almost convinced myself, but—fortunately—not quite.

I was also sometimes as happy as I would ever be. I had friends and ambitions. I hoped I would some time write a great poem, or a great novel, or perhaps both. The War would soon be over. The world, and the future, was all before me.

I was ready to rejoice at V-E Day, a fine sunny day in early May of 1945, walking down Queen Street on a shopping expedition with a group of friends, all carrying small Canadian ensigns that we had bought at Woolworths' or Zellers'. There was a happy bustle, but no riots, as there were in Halifax.

V-J Day was an anticlimax. My father had had a stroke after the dropping of the bomb on Hiroshima, and I was more concerned with his recovery than with public events. However, I went by myself, on what I remember as a dark, cloudy afternoon, to the service at the cenotaph, and wrote a rather bitter little poem about the "platitudes" with which the public figures there thanked the dead.

> The mayor at the cenotaph
> Speaks hopefully of lasting peace,
> While Time, the all-devouring, winks
> One eyelid, lolling at his ease.

So I wrote. Was I as cynical about the future as this sounds? Perhaps not, but my optimism was at least muted. In any case, the Second World War was never "the war to end war." That was 1914-1918.

Unlike Jane Marchant, the protagonist of my novel *The Sisters,* I attended university for another year after the War, received my BA in the spring of 1946, and went on to Graduate School at Radcliffe College (Harvard) that fall. My father was unable to work after his stroke, but the Army continued to pay him his salary for a year or so. He went on gentle walks, stopping on his way down town to sit on a bench in the Carleton Street graveyard. Sometimes I sat with him there, watching the pigeons watch the squirrels as they hopped along the path. It was an old graveyard, and nobody was buried in it any longer. In such a place, death seems natural rather than frightening. My father quoted his favourite Elegy by Thomas Gray. I quoted Hardy's lines about the burial of Drummer Hodge under "foreign constellations." We thought our separate thoughts.

I realize that I'm the same age now as my father was then.

Collage
(Dedicated to George Bowering)

The title "A Collage of Life and Dreams About My Father," came to me in a dream, and makes me think that dreams are not necessarily so truly inspired as the prophets thought they were. It sounds awkward. Awake, I could surely do better. I was also told in the dream that I was to write seven or perhaps eight stories about my father. One of the stories was to be "My Father Goes Fishing." I could write one a week, and in two months I would have completed a book. Even in my dream I knew better than that. Maybe one story, I thought. When I woke up, the time was 6.30 AM, too early to get up. I wrote the title on the memo pad provided by the hotel and went back to sleep.

I was in a hotel-room in Vancouver—the Georgia Hotel, as a matter of fact. Perhaps that's why I thought I should dedicate the story (anti-story or whatever it is) to George. Also, I had bought *Craft Slices* at Duthies' Bookstore and had thought to myself, "How clever to write a book in bits and pieces like that. I should do it some time." George and my father do share an initial. They are (were?) both tall. They both tell (told) jokes.

There was nothing special about my hotel-room in the Georgia Hotel that would make me think of my father. His mother's family did come from the South, but from Virginia, not from Georgia. It was an ordinary rectangular room with a bed and a desk and a television set. I had watched a television program on the invention of clocks. Clocks might make me think of time past, and the nature of time, and therefore of my parents.

There were two framed prints in the hotel-room, silkscreens, I think. One was of a bird in a flowering tree; the other was of a flowering tree without a bird in it. Of course birds and flowering trees make one think of poems by Yeats or Housman or Shelley or Rilke. Or Browning or Bowering. I think my father once brought me a spray of apple blossom with the rain still on it. I was a child of six or seven. He must have picked it near the house. Maybe a wind had blown down a branch of apple blossom. Or was it lilac? Or both at different times.

There were pink blossoms like those in the prints, come to think of it, on my father's shaving-mug. I watched him shave when I was three or four. He shaved in the kitchen, I think, because there was no bathroom. I loved all that foam on his face. I loved him.

26

What is the first time I remember my father? (Does it matter? To remember "the first time" of anything is to think the second of third time was less important. Anyhow, he saw me before I was able to see him, I suppose.)

Why can't people remember what they saw as babies? Is it because memory doesn't exist until language exists? Until I say, "There's Daddy with soap on his face"?

The first time I think I saw my father he is walking across the bedroom floor toward a bed in which I lie in my mother's arms. It's morning, before breakfast. My mother's long hair is braided down her back. She is wearing a flannel nightgown. My father is carrying a cookie in one hand, a round fat brown ginger cookie. He is winking at me and holding the cookie aloft—like a wafer in a monstrance, I think now, though I hadn't seen either a wafer or a monstrance then. I reach out toward the cookie. "Oh, Jack," my mother says, "you'll spoil her breakfast."

It was like my father to tempt me with cookies before breakfast, and like my mother to consider the necessity of a proper breakfast first, good thick oatmeal with lots of milk, boiled eggs in the big egg dish in the shape of a hen on its nest. Cookies are for later, my mother thought. (But she had made them.)

However, this is a collage of life and dreams about my father, not my mother. (How can I separate my father from my mother? They didn't believe in divorce.)

DREAMS: ONE

There were other dreams, before the one in which I was given a title.

Here is one, from some time last month:

"I dream I'm living in a house with my parents. I go out early in the morning to take a walk. There is a mist, something with a C—? A Corot or a Constable mist? It's a Sunday morning, but I'm thinking of visiting a bookstore. I would like to walk in a lane that is a short cut, but am afraid it might be too dangerous and lonely in the mist. I walk up stone stairs, like those crossing the railway track at George Street in Fredericton, but find the stairs difficult. I think, 'If it's difficult to walk uphill, you may be on the way downhill.' I see old Mrs. Crossman—or is it myself?—as an old woman on the stairs, but at the same time I am a young girl of perhaps sixteen walking along with an open book in my hand, in a hurry to get home before my parents come downstairs."

How all times and places come together, as if one time were pasted on top of another. I am sixteen, I am old as the hills. I am walking on a Sunday morning in Sussex or Sackville or Fredericton or Vancouver or through a London fog. Miss Smith in Sackville kept her bookstore open on Sunday. She had been in Spain during the Spanish Civil War. She had visited Russia. She was old and eccentric and some people avoided her, but she kept a marvellous bookstore. She made tea for her favourites, of whom I was one. I met the younger Lawren Harris in her store, and wondered how he felt about his father. I've just been to see his father's later paintings in the Vancouver Art Gallery. The only sunlight in Vancouver, I think. Will light come to me with that dazzlement in my extreme old age?

Two walks in Sussex when I was sixteen. One, a Sunday morning when I got up at a some absurd hour in June and walked in the mist and sunrise before coming home to breakfast and walking out to church again with my parents. I heard my father saying to my mother, "Oh, to be sixteen again. I suppose she'll write a poem about it."

And perhaps I did. I don't remember.

Another walk, a return home from school in the afternoon. I met my father, who had come to tell me, "Aunt Becky is dead." Aunt Becky was my mother's aunt, my favourite of all my mother's relatives. She was the last of her generation. It was autumn, the leaves were falling. Or perhaps I just remember it that way. If I hunted up the obituary, I might find it was spring. But I think of a mellow, warm autumn, years later. Victoria at Thanksgiving: a beautiful woman has just been murdered, though all we know at the moment is that she is missing. It is one of the serenest, most gracious October days I ever remember, and yet there is that suspense, a waiting for the confirmation of death. Another death.

What has that to do with my father? He died in autumn too, in September 1959. The telephone rang all day in the wrong room in a university residence, and I didn't get the call because the occupants of the room were away for the weekend. There was a telegram in the morning: *Father passed away. Funeral Wednesday.*

I wasn't at his funeral: it was too far, I couldn't make it in time.

Well, and what does that matter, now that all these years have passed? Why do I still feel the pain?

My father was a hypochondriac who was always going to die next month. Whenever I took a train or bus out of town, he would say, "When you come back I may not be here."—"Don't say things like that," I would say, or my mother would say. "Of course you'll be here." But the last time I left he didn't, for once, foretell his death. We both knew it was coming. I think he held death off by an act of will until I had gone, so that I wouldn't have to watch him die.

He had had a series of strokes, was lying in bed with a broken hip. He was as thin and fragile as a piece of mended, broken china. His eyes were as blue as when I was a child. I held his beautiful, wasted hand with its blue veins, fingered the gold ring with his initials, "F.J.B." (So I had held it when I was six, when I was seven, when I was nine.)

From the upstairs window we looked down at the white Catholic church just below us. We had quarrelled about religion at one time, my parents and I (especially my mother and I) but now we weren't quarrelling. I wasn't attending any church myself. I felt my heart closed against churches because they caused argument and bitterness. I thought perhaps my father would at least be pleased that I wasn't going to Mass, which he considered a superstitious rite. But perhaps he was worried because he felt that I had closed something off, had shut myself in.

What was it, exactly, that he said to me then? I should have written it down. Now I want to know. "There is a spirit," I think he said. "There is a God. You mustn't lose faith. The forms don't matter, the churches don't matter, it's the spirit."

I guess, when I think of it, you could call him an eighteenth-century deist or a nineteenth-century pantheist. "It's all a mystery," he had often said. He belonged to the Church of England and liked the prayers, or some of them, but I don't think he set store by creeds or sacraments or the 39 articles of religion. My mother, who had been brought up a Baptist, worried about beliefs. She also worried about actions, more than my father did. They were so different, and I loved them both. I could never choose between them. Sometimes I think I'm still trying to choose.

Could I, for instance, have chosen to write "A Collage of Life and Dreams About My Mother"? She would have liked something more orderly, wouldn't she? But how do I know that? After all, they did choose each other. If they, who were so different, could live together more or less happily, why can't I accommodate both their spirits in mine?

DREAMS: TWO

"I am brought to the front step of a very large house, a mansion. There is a broad sweep of a verandah or patio with a great hammock or perhaps a windowseat—something like a throne—in which a man is sitting, I think the Chairman of the Geography Department, whose name is Don or John. He is a tall man with a beard. (Don Juan? God? My father?) Behind him there is a backdrop of mountains and ocean, an evening sky with stars. I say, 'This is absolutely my favourite view. Can't we stay here?' He agrees about its beauty, asks me to come and sit beside him. It's slightly chilly outside, though very beautiful."

Hesitations at the door of one of the many mansions?

Was my father a Don Juan? He liked pretty women, but as far as I know he was always faithful to my mother. She was jealous of him, of course. She was even, at one point, jealous of me. I remember a summer when they were staying with me in Ottawa. He used to ask me to make a pot of tea for him in the late afternoon. Mother had always made the tea. Now he seemed to like the way I made it. One day she snapped, "No, I don't want a cup of tea. And," she glared at me, "don't think I don't know what you want to do!"

I was astonished, standing there on the front verandah holding the tray with the teapot and cookies. "What do you think I want to do?" I asked. I thought perhaps she had gone crazy.

But when I was a child she encouraged me to be Daddy's Girl. When I was six or so she made me a red dress. I remember putting it on for the first time, turning round and round in it, looking at myself in the mirror. "Now you'll be Daddy's red rose," my mother said. And I went dancing round the house singing, "I'm Daddy's red rose, I'm Daddy's red rose." When my father came home from work, I was waiting at the front gate for him, calling out to him, "Daddy, I'm your red rose."

"So you are," he said, and lifted me up in the air and whirled me around his head. "My rosebud."

There was my history professor at university, too. In the summer, he used to sit on a hammock on his front verandah reading and writing. He wrote poems; he was a friend of Earle Birney; he had read everything. He called me in when I walked by on the street, and I took a fat roll of poems out of my purse, where I put them just in case I saw him. I sat on a garden chair near him while he swung back and forth in the hammock, reading my poems, now and then making a comment.

"Better," he might say. "At least you've got rid of 'Verdant' and 'O Thou.' "

He was a god of sorts to me. He gave me a view of poetry and history. He wasn't, however, tall or bearded, like the figure in the dream. He was slight, rather delicate, always immaculately dressed, unflawed. My private nickname for him, which I don't remember sharing with anyone, was the Porcelain Prince, from a central character in a long fairy tale I used to tell myself when I was seven or eight. He had no children. At this point I half-wished I had been his daughter. At this point I was ashamed of my father (though of course I was ashamed of being ashamed). When I was a little girl, I had thought my father was very clever and knew everything. (He had read most of Dickens' novels. He could recite Gray's "Elegy in a Country Churchyard.") But by the time I was in university I knew that there were many things he didn't know. There were words he mispronounced. He said "Between you and I." His jokes no longer seemed funny. (When we moved to Needham Street, he said, "Of course you can remember it. We need ham every hour.") His mouth hung open; most of his teeth were bad. He was afraid of dentists.

Still, it was my father—my real father—who sent off my first poem to a newspaper to be published when I was twelve years old. He didn't tell me he had sent it away, but came in triumphantly the day it was published with half a dozen copies of the paper tucked under his arm. He was as excited by print as I was. I was pleased that he was pleased, and yet already I was beginning to be embarrassed by him. He ought not to express his delight so simply and directly. He ought not to be such a boy when he was in his fifties.

GHOST STORIES

I'm staying now in a small motel in Victoria, have been here for a week, expect to stay another two weeks. I have a room which is living-room—dining-room—kitchen all in one. There is also a bedroom, where I can maintain my habit of dreaming. There is a painting over the desk in the living-room: deserted farm shed in the background with a red wheel leaning against it; an old grey (not red) wheelbarrow in the foreground; white wheels of daisies. The red wheel of the sun is not shown, its presence merely implied by the light. All the wheels rhyme with one another. A scene that might be inhabited by ghosts, perhaps ghosts of small children rolling hoops.

I sit curled up on the orange-and-brown sofa in the living-room, reading over what I've written. Why did the dream say I was to write "stories," or at least a story? This is not a story. A story has a beginning, a middle and an end. A story has a direction. A story has a theme. It has a conflict you can recognize. There is a climax, maybe a recognition scene, a reversal. A story has a mystery. A story is like "The Cask of Amontillado" or *Oliver Twist*. A story is like the narratives my father practised and told over and over again, "My Night in the Haunted House," "The Time I Was Lost in the Demoiselle Creek Caves," "My First Vote," "The Day I Enlisted in the Army," "My Feud with the Old Senator." If I could retell those stories just as he told them, my father would appear in them as lovable and folksy, a great entertainer. But I can't tell stories in his way.

The one I used to ask him to retell most often when I was a child—"My Night in the Haunted House"—was not really typical of his stories, for it was anticlimactic. He did try to build it up, gave a long account of the old house in Hopewell that was said to be haunted, the lights seen in the windows at night, the refusal of people to rent or buy it. My father, then a boy of sixteen or so, accepted a dare to spend the night by himself in the old Appleby place. The house was still partly furnished, but the furniture was covered with sheets to keep off the dust. In one corner of the old parlour was a bulky shrouded piano. It was beside the piano that my father chose to settle down for the night, stretched on the carpet, his head on his folded jacket. "Come on, Ghosts," he said to the room, and felt a breeze from the window, where the pane was broken, blowing across his face. But it was only a summer breeze, not even very cold.

He lay awake for a long time, listening to rustlings that might be the rustlings of mice. The leisurely summer twilight turned to total darkness. Once, when he heard a tap-tap against the window, he struck a match and looked out. Nothing but a branch in the wind. He lay down again. A flutter of wings. Some kind of bird, he supposed, perhaps a bat. He struggled to keep awake: if a ghost arrived, he wanted to be on hand to witness it. But somehow, in spite of all his efforts, sleep overcame him. When he awoke, sunshine was streaming in through the window, birds were cheeping away in the big pine tree outside. He had a crick in his neck and a numb leg from lying on the floor, but otherwise was unharmed.

Did I ask him to repeat this story so often because I liked the rational ending, the reassuring failure of the ghosts to appear? Did I hope that some time he would change the ending and say that in fact he was awakened by an invisible pianist playing some ghostly waltz? Or did I feel that a ghost had indeed been raised by the telling of the story, the ghost of my father at sixteen, nearly 30 years before I was born? Ghost of a sixteen-year-old boy with tow hair and bright blue eyes, stretching and yawning sleepily in the morning sunshine, back there in the reign of Victoria.

I'm never quite sure whether I'm terrified of ghosts or whether I long to meet them, provided they're the right ones. I don't want to call up the ghost of my Cousin Alex, who went for a walk in the woods and shot himself. Ghosts of those who died in anguish, unforgiven or unforgiving—those might be dangerous. But I can't imagine my father's ghost would be dangerous. "I'll come back from the other side and tell you what it's like," he used to joke, or perhaps promise. But he's never come back, at least to me. My mother said he appeared to her, but that was shortly before her own death, when she was having hallucinations and seeing birds in the bathtub.

Oh, there was one time I thought I felt his presence. The summer after he died, after I had visited my mother in Chipman, I took the bus from Chipman to Sackville. My father, I was convinced, sat beside me all the way to Sackville. Nobody else sat down beside me. Perhaps he was visible to the other passengers.

He had hoped his mother's ghost would appear to him after she died, but she never did, except sometimes in dreams, when she walked away from him, looking over her shoulder and calling, "Come, Johnnie, come."

My grandmother, according to my father, was a great teller of ghost stories. When my parents visited her shortly after they were married, she would spend the evening telling one of these stories. Then she would say to my mother, who was especially afraid of ghosts, "And now, Ethel, my dear, would you just go down to the cellar and bring us up a jar of preserves for our midnight supper?"

Did she carry a lamp or a lantern or a candle, walking carefully down the steps to the dark basement, full of night and shadows? There on the cobwebby shelves were jars of jam, preserves, pickles, jelly, chokecherry wine. She would pick something at random, her heart thudding wildly, and then make her way upstairs again to the warm kitchen and toast and tea. Once she was sure she saw a ghost near the shelves of preserves and dropped a jar and ran. The next morning she came down and cleaned the glass and the blood-red juice of strawberries off the cellar floor.

Perhaps it was to comfort my mother that my father began to tell the story, "My Night in the Haunted House."

DREAMS: THREE

"I arrive at a hotel or inn in a horse-drawn vehicle driven (from the train station? the ship?) by an employee of the inn. Am

35

wearing what seems to be a nineteenth-century costume, full silk or satin skirts, a bonnet. It's an inn I've visited before, and employees greet me in a friendly way. I hold up a key that I had accidentally taken with me on my former visit, say something about an umbrella. Later, the man who drove me to the inn waits on me at the dinner table. He wears some unusual costume—Scottish tartan, perhaps?"

I suppose these are invented ancestral ghosts from the past. My father's mother, Elizabeth Elston, came up to New Brunswick from Virginia with her parents after the American Civil War. She must've been a young woman. I would calculate she was born around 1840. She had a brother, my father's Uncle Henry, who was killed fighting for the Confederate side. My grandmother remembered being looked after as a child by a slave, a black mammy who accompanied the family to New Brunswick. My father never visited the South, but was always sentimental about it, and used to put me to sleep singing "Carry me back to Old Virginny." He adored his mother. My mother was fond of her, but also jealous of her, though she did not admit her jealousy until her own deathbed.

My father thought the Elstons were a Scottish family, but wasn't sure. His father's family was from Lincolnshire, but had been in North America since the *Mayflower*. My father was proud of that, though my mother was inclined to sniff. Why should people be proud of what was underground? Her father's family was United Empire Loyalist, but she never told us about them. Perhaps she didn't know. She knew about the Scotch-Irish immigrants who came later.

My father was, like me, the child of older parents. There were two older children who had died of scarlet fever; there was also a half sister, Nell, the daughter of my grandfather by an earlier marriage. Grandfather died when my father was a child of nine. There used to be an old tintype of my father at ten or so standing beside his mother, who was seated wearing widow's weeds, heavy black skirts, a hat with a black veil, though the veil was thrown back from her face. Clearly, at that point they were the most important people in the world for each other.

Still, they were often separated from each other when he was growing up. Grandmother worked as a nurse, and Jack was sent to live in Hopewell with his sister Nell and her husband. Hopewell and the rocky shore with its shells and samphire greens and the sound of waves—that was his Eden, though he missed his mother and the ghost of his father.

LUNCH AT LA PETITE COLOMBE

Today I have lunch with a friend. (I'll call her Laura, which isn't her name, but I need to call her something.) I tell her that I'm writing about my father. "Can you be honest about your father?" she asks.

"I think I can," I say. "In moderation. With some changes."

She tells me a story about her father. But that is her story. It would be good written down. She tells stories better than I do. "But I would feel it was a betrayal to write about my father," she says, though her story has made me like him.

But I don't think I feel it's a betrayal to write abut my parents, even though they mightn't like it if they were alive. It's my way of coming to terms with them, perhaps. Maybe my way of prolonging their existence, since I have no children.

"Did you get on well with your parents?" Laura asks. "Were you close to them? Did you have troubles with them?"

In conversation, when you answer a direct question, you always have to simplify. "Perhaps I was too close," I say. Certainly there was a period when I felt they moved in on my territory, that I had to push them back in order to breathe, had to keep them at arm's length. "I was too close and then maybe I was too distant."

I tell her the story of my mother and the tea. "But I was always very close to my mother when I was growing up," I say.

"I think I would always have been close to them both if it hadn't been for my temporary conversion to Catholicism. You couldn't expect old-fashioned New Brunswick Orangemen to approve of that."

"Was your father an Orangeman? Really?" (Laura leans over the table, her eyes bright. Perhaps she has never met an Orangeman.)

"Well, Dad did belong to the Orange Lodge, but in fact after initially blowing off steam he accepted it pretty well. It was my mother who had the most difficulty. Later, after they were both dead, I regretted it. No church or idea is as important as one human being. I should've gone to church with my mother if it made her happy."

"But she wouldn't have agreed with that, surely?"

"No, you're right. Dad would have, though."

I suppose Dad belonged to the Orange Lodge because, when was a young man, joining Lodges was something you did. In the country places in New Brunswick when he was growing up, all the men belonged either to the Orange Lodge or the Knights of Columbus. The two big social occasions of the summer were the Twelfth of July and the Priest's Picnic. I was taken to both as a child. The Twelfth of July was the more lavish of the two. There was a parade with a local farmer as King Billy on a white horse, commemorating the Battle of the Boyne. There was a pavilion where young couples danced to the tunes of local fiddlers. There was an endless supply of ice cream at five cents a cone for the children, as well as more substantial food, and Sussex ginger ale (the best kind) and tea for the grownups. Perhaps some of the men had something alcoholic to drink, but it wasn't visible. There were speeches, but I don't remember listening to them. People who think of the Orange Lodge as a group of bigots in Belfast would not understand my childhood association of it with the most beautiful picnic of the summer, perfect weather, wooden tables under green trees, young leaping dancers, the parade with the mythical king at its head and the lively music. No doubt there was a less idyllic side, but I didn't see it.

The Priest's Picnic was a quieter affair, but similar in a way. There wasn't a parade, as far as I remember, but there was dancing, and there were races and games for the children. My mother and I went with her Catholic aunt and cousins, Auntie Maggie and the rest, and we ate lunch with them from their baskets under a big maple tree. I was rather afraid of the priest when he came by, though he smiled at me and chatted with my mother and inquired about Aunt Maggie's rheumatism. I stayed very close to my mother, and put my hand out to touch her hand.

DREAMS: FOUR

This was one of my Vancouver dreams:

"Dream of being with a tour group. Arrangement for a group meal. It is laid out on long wooden benches, something like what I've seen in Sunday School picnics as a child: bread, meat, fish, cheese, perhaps wine or grape juice. A sort of communion? It's outdoors, outside an inn. Is it the opposite side from what was expected? I talk to the tour guide, a man."

Is the tour guide my father?

Any meal is a communion, I suppose. The crêpes I shared with Laura at La Petite Colombe. The ice cream cones and picnic lunches at the Twelfth of July picnic and the Priest's Picnic. Any meal is sacramental.

(A part of me says, "Come off it. You're being altogether too solemn.")

Is the cheese Kraft Slices? Probably not. Probably farmer's country cheddar.

MY FATHER GOES FISHING

If there is a mystery about that opening dream, it's the direction it gave to write a story "My Father Goes Fishing." So far as I know, my father never went fishing. He played baseball in his youth. He was always a strenuous walker. But he had no taste for hunting or fishing, though my brothers both did. I never went fishing myself, but I dimly remember as a small child playing at fishing with a toy rod and line, and pretending to bait the hook with angleworms that I had dug up from the garden and put in one of my father's old tobacco tins. So far as I remember, I never caught anything. There was an often-told family story of the elder of my brothers, as a small boy, having caught a salmon with his naked hands in the stream behind the house. He carried it home, still gasping for its life, and laid it on the kitchen table for my mother to clean and cook. "And we ate it for a week," she used to say.

But what did the dream mean when it asked me to write about my father going fishing? Is it that I myself was commanded to go fishing, to submerge myself in depths of dream or memory, back and back in time, and so to catch the fish, the sacred and healing fish? I wrote a poem once about the fish in the Book of Tobit, the fish from which Tobit or Tobias made a salve to cure his father's blindness. When the liver and entrails of the fish were burned, the smoke drove away the evil spell that had prevented Tobit's bride from making a happy marriage. But Tobit needed the help of an angel to catch the fish. Everyone knows—does everyone know?—that the fish was the great symbol of Christianity, that fish were painted on the walls of the catacombs.

If Saint John, my father's patron saint, did not go fishing, Saint Peter certainly did. God is a fisherman who hoicks us all in at last (so Jay Macpherson says).

Or you could say that the fish is a phallic symbol; or perhaps it's the fisherman's rod that is the phallic symbol. The fisherman's rod brings the new life of the foetus leaping like a small lively fish out of the waters of the womb.

Then my father went fishing when I was conceived, and how can I tell the story of my conception, since nobody has told it to me?

I was the fifth and youngest child of my parents. There were two brothers, two sisters, before me. When my mother knew she was pregnant, she was dismayed. She was 39, would be 40 by the time I was born. My father's little clothing store had gone bankrupt; he had had what he called a nervous breakdown; he had no job. How were they to manage?

But my parents loved one another. There must have been love at my conception, love and the desire to comfort. My mother decided that I was to be an artist and a musician. My father thought I would be a boy whom he would name James. Instead I was a girl, named for his dying mother and for the daughter of his commanding officer in the war, a young girl who had died of TB—consumption, they called it then— before she was twenty. Named for two ghosts.

NAMES

Names were sometimes a puzzle for a young child. My father was not only Papa and Daddy and Dad; he was Fred to most of his friends, Jack to his own mother and sister, F.J. to my brothers when they were being disrespectful. And of course Brewster or Mr. Brewster to more general acquaintances. Mother (Mamma, Mum) was also Ethel or Ef or Ethel May or Mrs. Brewster. Elizabeth is a name that contains four or five names, as I discovered at an early age from the nursery rhyme. My father also called me Jamie or Jim-Jam or Miss Muffet or (because I was little) Skimper. My mother sometimes called me Child or Pet. My sister Marion called me Cutest or Countess, or, if she was annoyed with me, Petunia. Nobody called me by my actual first name, Winifred. My brother Percy was Spike to his friends; my father sometimes called him John. My brother Cyril was Cy. Marion was usually just Marion, though she could be Molly. My sister Eleanor was sometimes Nell or Buster.

Everyone deserves at least two names, to indicate some of the many personalities contained in one body. Fred, I think, was my father's public personality, a lively extrovert, something of a joker; Jack or Johnnie was gentle, vulnerable, melancholy, given to worries, headaches, insomnia. If I've inherited some of my father's personality, it's mainly from John, not from Fred.

As a young woman, I didn't want to inherit my father's personality, particularly his melancholy. Once, in the days when I suffered especially from depression, when I was undergoing psychoanalysis, he tried to tell me how he coped with the same temperament. "If I get up in the morning feeling sad," he said, "I go and talk to people. I smile at them. I tell them a little joke. Then I begin to feel better myself, even if it's half pretence. I can get through the day."

"But I don't want only to get through the day," I cried. "I want to be really happy, not just to endure. I don't want to be like you."

I saw him wince, and realized my unintentional cruelty. And after all, I know now, his advice was fairly good. Who has the right to expect more than the ability to endure, to get through the day? I expected too much from life then: perfect love rather than a pleasant acquaintance and a joke over coffee; perfect happiness rather than acceptance of being human. Still—resignation and acceptance are the virtues (some might say the vices) of 65, not of 25. If I had a daughter, she would probably argue with me now, say angrily, "Life isn't just something to put up with."

Still, accept life as something to put up with, and all sorts of small things become pleasurable: red tulips in a vase on the kitchen counter; the taste of apples; a conversation with an old Ukrainian woman from the prairies encountered in the Museum tea shop; a picture in the tea shop of three fish, one with a human head.

Why was the word "collage" given to me in the first dream? How is this account a collage? Are dreams pasted on top of life, thought, memory, or is it the other way around? Are the dreams the true base and the factual information what is added? Are they equally important?

> "*Collage.* 1919 [Fr. lit. 'pasting'] An abstract form of art in which photographs, pieces of string, etc., are placed in juxtaposition and glued to the pictorial surface; such a work of art."

There is a Greek word *kólla* that means "glue."

DREAMS: FIVE

"A dream of being on the psychoanalyst's couch, or, rather, of getting up from it. I am wearing a half-slip, am about to put on slacks, I think, though it may be a skirt."

I did not, of course, actually strip to my slip, or my half-slip, on the psychoanalyst's couch. Perhaps I thought of psychoanalysis as a mental stripping. Perhaps it seems as if I were stripping in telling this story. (Not completely, of course.)

No doubt I talked about my father during the psychoanalysis. How I loved my father. How I was sometimes ashamed of him.

QUESTION IN LONDON, ONTARIO

"Was there much incest in rural New Brunswick when you were growing up?"

Somebody in London, Ontario asked me that question a few years ago. I gathered that there was quite a bit in

Southwestern Ontario.

"Not much, as far as I know," I told him.

When we lived in Sussex, my mother came home once from a meeting of the Church Guild, shocked because she had heard of a family out in the country where there was a confused incestuous situation, a young woman who had had children by both her father and her brother.

I suppose incest and child molestation are about the only taboos left, of all the many taboos that were operating when I was a child.

Any incest in our family was only emotional. I was not molested as a child except by other children who were not related to me. But that is another story and has nothing to do with my father.

DREAMS: SIX

"A dream of visiting my father, who is old and sick and living in a shack with his second wife, whose name is Marion. When I come out of the house, rain is pouring down on me, on my uncovered head, but I don't seem to mind."

Of course my father never had a second wife. Marion is the name of my sister, now dead. It is also the name of my brother Cy's second wife. (My brother died a few years ago.) It was the name of my great-grandmother Elston. And it is the name of the widow of a former lover of mine.

Is the man in the dream father, brother, lover, all of whom I saw old and sick?

None of them died in a shack.

"The soul's dark cottage, battered and decayed/ Lets in new light through chinks that time hath made." I memorized that in high school, or perhaps in my first year at university.

Did the battered, decaying bodies of those old men let in wisdom? Am I the soul walking out of the wrecked house into the rain of a new spring? Or am I dreaming of the rain of love

("O Westron Wind...")?

Rain of love, reign of love.

The seafood restaurant where I had lunch the other day had a reproduction of that Botticelli painting of Venus rising from the sea, naked except for her long hair.

Doves sometimes hover around the head of Venus. The dove is also the symbol of the Holy Ghost. *La Petite Colombe.* Symbols converge upon one another.

Of course I loved all three of those men. Not to mention the Marions, mother-sister figures, other selves.

My sister Marion, like my grandmother, used to love to tell ghost stories. She told stories of a house where the family had lived before I was born. At night the piano in the living-room downstairs would play by itself, when everybody was safely tucked in bed upstairs. Draughts of cold air blew over their faces on summer evenings, draughts of a peculiar spiritual iciness. The covers on my sister's bed would rise of their own accord and hover in the air a few feet above them. (This happened also, Marion said, to my brothers, sleeping in the next room.) Sometimes a ghost became visible, a bearded man in long underwear; a woman in a gauzy white shawl.

I remember, when I was three or four years old, waking up after Marion had told me ghost stories and seeing a closet with its door open, spectral clothes shining in the moonlight. Why was I sleeping by myself? I crept out of my bed, padded on bare feet into my parents' room, slipped under the covers with them. I woke up almost smothering, clasped between them in their sleeping embrace.

I wanted then to be close to all of them. Perce carried me around on his shoulders. I sat on Cy's chest and thumped him with my doll and told him I would marry him when I grew up. On Sunday mornings I got into bed with Marion and Eleanor and looked at the funny papers with them, Little Orphan Annie and Bringing Up Father and the Toonerville Folks and Our Boarding House. On the days I loved my family, I felt sorry for Annie, because she didn't have a father or mother or brothers or sisters. On the days I didn't love them, I wondered if I might be an orphan too.

DREAMS: SEVEN

"My brother Cy and I are sitting together at a kitchen table. His wife isn't in the room. We talk of cooking: is it a waste of time to potter about preparing food? I say to him (or perhaps he says to me), 'You might as well enjoy yourself. Nothing you do will last 500 years.'"

I don't know what work he is thinking of. Of course I think of writing. I know also that I've changed the time from a hundred years to 500. Some writing—Chaucer's, maybe?—lasts 500 years. A house—a Canadian house, anyhow—is lucky to last a hundred. Most machinery lasts less than a human lifetime. Some objects—Christmas tree ornaments, for example—may last only a few days.

It's an echo of something my father used to say: "It'll all be the same a hundred years from now." Meaning, of course, that we'd all be dead in a hundred years, even the youngest of us, so why should we agonize about a skinned knee, or a broken leg, or a prize not won, or a lost job or a lost friend? Of course, he did agonize himself about these things.

Nothing lasts, and yet everything lasts. All the matter of the universe must have been present, concentrated together, at the instant of the Big Bang.

If one thinks of the billions of years of the universe, and the great dance of the planets, even the returnings of Halley's Comet (which my father saw in 1910, and his father must have seen in 1835), then any one human life seems a glow-worm in the dark, a tiny flickering gleam. And of what importance is my father, or what he accomplished, or what he didn't accomplish? But my father was alive, unlike the planets or the comets. As I write I think, Perhaps he may guide my pen.

I don't know why I remember at this moment a story I read

in an old school reader—not my own, but my sister's. It was Samuel Johnson (was it Samuel Johnson?) going as a grown man to a place where he had refused to accompany his father selling books in a market stall. The boy had been ashamed of his father, of his father's position in the market; the grown man had sat all day, his bare head open to sun and wind, doing penance for that shame. To do justice to his father, an honourable poor man who earned his living in a way the boy had felt was beneath him.

Is this what I really want to do in this story: to do penance for being ashamed of my father?

I think of him sometimes as the White Knight in *Alice in Wonderland,* who was always falling off his horse. And yet he was a knight, truly, and protected Alice as much as he was able to.

It was my father who carried me down from the roof of the house when I had climbed up the ladder but had been frightened to climb down. It was my father who walked out in a snow storm to meet me coming home from school and carried me home in his arms.

But when he lost his job in Bert Smith's store in Minto, in the early days of the Depression, he couldn't get another. He tried to farm, and we nearly starved. He tried to sell magazine subscriptions and mail-order made-to-measure suits from Tip-Top Tailors. Who needed suits, unless a man expected to be married or buried? For that mattter, the old suit would do to be buried in.

When the war came, he did get a job as a janitor and nightwatchman. And he and my mother helped me to pay my way through university.

Is there anything he did that has lasted? Nothing but his children, and two of them are dead. Quite a few grandchildren, not all of them creditable. I have a nephew in Victoria just now, in the Navy, and we spent an evening not long ago talking about family skeletons. We could spend another such evening. My nephew thinks he would like to be a writer. He says he has lots to write about. Parents or brother or voyages?

Of course, I've sometimes talked over my parents with my brothers and sisters, as I talked over my brothers and sisters with my parents.

"F.J. couldn't swear," Cy said of my father. "Even when he was really angry, he could only swear like a little boy."

Not that I ever heard either of my brothers swear, either. Only my sisters.

"He was good with children," Eleanor said. "Not strict like Mum."

"He was stronger than you might think," Marion said. "He wasn't afraid of death. He never complained. We always thought Mum was stronger, but I don't know if she really was." (Maybe they were both strong, I think.)

My brother Perce is deaf. "We're talking about Dad," I wrote on a scrap of paper for him.

"Pop. I miss talking to him," Percy said. (He looked at my father's ring, which he was wearing.)

And it's true they had long conversations, sometimes with gestures, sometimes on paper.

DREAMS: EIGHT

"A dream that I am helping my father, who is lame, from one room to another, where there is a couch for him to rest. My mother is also present. He calls out for her to bring some clippings, or perhaps a scrapbook, for me to see. There are clippings of poems from magazines. One of them has a line drawn through to cancel it out. There is also one by the son of a friend, and I think perhaps this must especially interest him, but in fact it seems the clipping is really of the poem on the other side of the page. This poem appears to be one written by Sir Charles Roberts in old age to his young second wife. However, the poem is not actually by Roberts; it is a poem pretending to be said by Roberts. 'I is not I.' The manner is rather like

Great-Aunt Rebecca

Cyril & Frances: brother & sister-in-law

Frederick & Ethel: father & mother

Percy & Ada: brother & sister-in-law

Marion: older sister

With Cyril

At six

Today

that of W.H. Davies, I think. Should I write this poem, I wonder?"

What am I to make of this dream? Clearly, both my father and my mother are needed in the presentation of the scrapbook. My father also needs my help to move from room to room.

Is what I am writing a scrapbook of prose poems instead of a story? Prosaic prose poems?

Once my old lover said to me, over dinner in a restaurant, "Why do you suppose that young woman married Charles Roberts anyway? There's some mystery there. Did she want to be Lady Roberts? Did she want to be the wife of a distinguished poet? There were better poets around who were nearer her age."

"Maybe she wasn't bright enough to know they were better poets," I said. "Maybe there wasn't any mystery. The Roberts men were attractive to women. Maybe she was in love."

Still, there's always a mystery about love. Of any kind, for lovers, friends, brothers, parents, children.

Why did I think I might write a poem in the voice of Charles Roberts speaking to his wife rather than in the voice of the wife speaking to her husband? Is the "I" of Charles Roberts a greater disguise for me than the "I" of Joan Roberts would be?

MAPS

My friend Laura arranged a lunch with two other women. One of them is also a poet, both of them teach. They talked about making maps or charts of poems or stories, paintings, music, to show their structure.

Could this story be mapped?

"I think life has a structure with recurring images," I said. "Is life the product of an artist?"

"Oh, it is, it is," Laura said.

I saw a fish, a dove and the sun together in a painting from Lapland in the Provincial Museum. This dove was the dove of peace, with a green branch in its mouth.

Where was Noah?

FINAL DREAM IN VICTORIA

"A dream of a man in rags, a tramp or jester, who wishes to marry the princess. She refuses, but he asks for permission to draw on the blackboard. He draws two circles side by side with human figures in them. As he points toward them with his pointer, they become three, but three in one, as in a joined shamrock or clover leaf or trefoil. They are (it is) also illuminated, as if in stained-glass, and glows with brilliant colours. The princess decides—or perhaps her guardians decide—that the marriage is after all possible. I awake. It is St. Patrick's Day."

The old fairy story of the prince disguised as a gypsy-tramp who marries the princess?

St. Patrick demonstrating the nature of the trinity?

The mystery of father, mother and child, as triple unity or united three?

My father: jester in rags, despised prince, saint, priest, magician, teacher, artist, lover. St. John, St. George, St. Patrick.

Or have I been dreaming all along about death, the farmer-lover, prince-in-disguise, whose scythe may resemble a magician's rod or a fisherman's rod? Death, who divides and dismembers, but who may perhaps unify? Death, who sits at the door of mansions with expanding views? Who carries travellers to his inn and waits on them at table?

CHIPMAN—The death of Frederick J. Brewster, 81, a former resident of Fredericton, occurred at his home in Chipman after a lengthy illness. He moved to Chipman two years ago.

He is survived by his wife, the former Ethel May Day of Chipman; two sons, Percy S. of Centreville and Cyril P. of Fort William, Ont.; three daughters, Mrs. Marion Cameron of Fredericton, Mrs. Ernest West of Minto and Miss Elizabeth, of Bloomington, Indiana.

Service was held at the Anglican Church, with Rev. J.H. Secord officiating.

IN MEMORIAM

BREWSTER: In loving memory of a dear husband and father, Frederick J. Brewster, who passed away 27 Sept., 1959.

Fondly remembered by wife Ethel and family.

Twenty-seven years after his death another In Memoriam: Still fondly remembered by the few remaining.

Jonah's whale a metaphor for the tomb?

Have I gone fishing within the depth of the whale to bring back my father alive? And those others swallowed since then?

INHERITANCE

1

As a child I overheard my deaf father
talking to himself, wondering
where the next meal was coming from, saying
"All's lost," saying
"What will we do?"
Saying, "They'd be better off without me."

And I followed him about dumbly,
wishing to say "I love you"
fearing where he might walk
or what he might do
wishing to make him successful
brilliant and admired,
and not this shabby man
with mended trousers
and scuffed shoes
stumbling apologetically about the house.

2

He was a good man, my father,
a childlike man,
never given to violence, afraid of blood,
afraid of hurting others, a gentle man;
yet I think I was ashamed of him a little
because he never won in life,
also because he tried to comfort himself
by pretending to despise those who prospered,
and because he talked too loudly
and repeated the same jokes many times.

But I could never cut him out of myself,
my argumentative, mild father,
arrogant and timid.

Sometimes lately
I find I also repeat the same jokes.

3

My mother was always hunting for four-leaf clovers,
and, since her eyes were quick, she found many.
They were stuffed in all her books and Bibles,
but she complained to me once
that they did not bring her luck.

I repeated her words to a neighbour
and she rebuked me later.

"Never tell anyone outside the family,"
she warned me then,
"that any of us don't think we are lucky."

4

Green was my mother's favourite colour,
colour of grass and hope.
All her life she wanted
a green velvet dress
and never had one.

Victorian Interlude

A sunny afternoon in Victoria. I should be out walking, but have already been walking and my feet are tired. I sit at my small round table in this temporary perch of mine looking down the hill at the nineteenth-century castle towers of the Empress Hotel. To get a really good view of Douglas Street, leading down to the Empress, I have to stand up and walk over to the end window. There I can see the cars going by, an old couple walking along the sidewalk with matching canes, a young boy bouncing eagerly up the hill toward me. There is one bus, then another.

It's not as warm as Victoria sometimes is at this time of year. When I came in from the airport on Tuesday I could see snow along the way. But the snow is gone, and there is green grass. And today, sunshine.

My small apartment is a corner one, so that the large window on the other side looks out on Beacon Hill Park, where there are more walkers, a man on a bicycle, a blue-clad jogger and a woman in a red coat sitting on a park bench. Now she stands up, and I see that she too is lame, and walks partly with the aid of a cane and partly supported by a man—or is it a woman?—in brown, who keeps step patiently with her. Gradually, painfully, they are climbing up the winding path out of my sight.

I came here intending to write. Three years ago, in the motel around the corner, I wrote about my father. I examined my dreams, I called up my memories. I tacked them together, layer on layer. I thought perhaps now I might do the same for my mother. Is that what I want? I have received no directions in a dream, as I did before.

Perhaps if I put the kettle on for tea (my mother's favourite drink) I might hear a voice. She used to tell fortunes in the tea leaves: you will meet a tall stranger, you will travel to Australia, you will receive money in the mail, you will shed some tears. It's from my mother that I picked up my small irrational superstitions: the new moon brings good luck, unless seen through glass; a four-leaf clover is lucky; opals are unlucky; if you have to come back for something after leaving the house, sit down and count seven before leaving again. On the other hand, she disapproved of playing-cards, though someone told her fortune in the cards when she was a young girl. I don't know if she knew the Tarot pack. Was she the high priestess, with her veil and her book? Was she the queen-empress, throned and sceptred, her feet on the crescent moon? Was she Strength, curbing the lion's jaws? Was she the magician, who

55

can be either male or female, though the card shows him as male? Perhaps she might have liked the Tarot, if she hadn't been warned against it. God's picture books, maybe, rather than the devil's.

CARDS: THE HIGH PRIESTESS (LA PAPESSE)

My first thought of her is as high priestess. In the card, the lady is seated in a chair with one arm resting on a carved sphinx. A partly open book is on one knee, two keys on the other. Her head is veiled, though her face is not, and over the veil is a golden tiara, with a crescent moon on top. There is another white veil behind her. Blue she wears, with a red cloak over it, a touch of green, a border of yellow. (Sky and sunshine, grass and earth? The white mist of cloud and fog and rain?)

My mother was the first to hold me up to the window to see the moon, with the white clouds sailing before its face, a marvellous object. It was she who taught me to pray "Now I lay me down to sleep," and I remember kneeling in the fat white bed, tumbling over on uncertain knees, repeating the words to her. ("If I should die before I wake." What did that mean? Did I ask her? Did she try to explain?) It was she who read the Bible aloud at night, while I, as the youngest, sat on her lap. She gave me the book of Bible stories from which I learned my letters. She read aloud from Grimms' fairytales and Mother Goose. My father introduced me to the newspaper—Lindbergh, Jack Dempsey, the king and the prime minister. Later he introduced me to Dickens and Tennyson. My sisters provided me with the funny papers, Tillie the Toiler, Mutt and Jeff and the Katzenjammer Kids. But my mother introduced me to the Sacred Scriptures: the Bible, the fairytales, romantic novels. It was while sitting on my mother's lap as she turned the pages of Shakespeare that I saw *The Tempest* illustrated and wished to read it, and Hamlet holding the skull in his hands, and a procession of angels greeting Catherine of Aragon. And, curled up beside her on the bed on a Sunday afternoon when I was six or seven, I read along with her as she sank into one of those trashy (no doubt) romances she loved, with earls and countesses and villains and heroes and purity.

I always carry a few books with me when I travel, often books I've read a number of times and feel I can read again with pleasure. This time I brought *Pilgrim's Progress, The Blithedale Romance* and Wordsworth's *Prelude. Pilgrim's Progress* is the only one I'm sure my mother read. When she was a child, it was one of the few books she was allowed to read on Sunday, when only godly books might be read. Probably she read *Blithedale,* too. I know she had read some of Hawthorne, and those small poems by Wordsworth that everybody reads in school.

CARDS: MAGICIAN

I have reversed the order of high priestess and magician, for I think the cards should be chosen at random.

My mother the magician. The magician is priestly too, with his altar on which are the chalice and the sword and the gold coin (or is it a wafer?) marked with a cross. How clever the magician is to transform this to that. Flour and sugar and apples are transformed into apple pie, and the pie is changed to a little girl's apple cheeks. I remember the small saucer pies my mother made for me and how magic they seemed. It required pure sorcery, miracles of bread and fishes, to keep a family fed in the days of the Great Depression. My mother's magic powers were sometimes strained.

Is magic a trick or a miracle? Does it require faith or merely skill? Both, perhaps?

Too dominant a magician she was sometimes, too conscious of the rod of power. "Obey," she said. "I want you to obey me." Parents are to be obeyed and respected. That is what she was taught by her own parents.

Is the sword the tongue? She did not need to use physical punishments. Her tongue was enough. And yet I am at a loss to remember any really harsh words, at any rate back there when I was a child. "If you love me," she said, "do what I say." Is love a weapon?

Saturday, 25 February

A darker day today, though there are glimpses of blue sky. Across the street in the park I see the same blue-clad jogger running down the hill. A man with a hunched back is walking up it, rather briskly, with his arms behind his back. On another path there is a woman in blue with a pink hat. She has a cane, but does not seem to be lame.

I have bought daffodils, and they stand in a green vase on top of my small table. Beside them is a bowl of oranges, reminding me of childhood, when oranges came only for Christmas, wrapped in crinkly pink tissue paper and tucked into the toe of a stocking. The days when my father was king and my mother was queen.

CARDS: EMPRESS AND EMPEROR

The empress precedes the emperor. She wears a crown, haloed with the stars of the zodiac. She is winged and bears a sceptre in one hand, and, on the other side, a red shield with a white eagle. A lily grows beside her. One foot is on the crescent moon.

The emperor is helmeted and sceptred. He holds a round green ball, the earth, in his hand, and a red flower grows at his feet. His eagle is a dark eagle.

White lily, white eagle, angel wings. When I was a little girl, I thought of my mother as totally good. Later I realized she had her dark side, that she could be narrow and bitter and

58

angry.

Yet when I try to imagine her now, I see her first in white, as she appeared in her wedding picture. She wears a white muslin dress that she sewed herself, with puffed sleeves and a narrow waist. Her black hair is swept back from her forehead and crowned with a white bow. Her dark eyes are large and serious. Her mouth is sweet but firm. She is in her early twenties, but looks perhaps nineteen. Of course I never saw her so young. She was over 40 when I was born. But I thought her then very beautiful, and I still believe she was.

I don't know why I think now of a time when I was about four years old. Short hair was in fashion, and my mother's friend Martha had visited for the day and cut my mother's hair, "shingled" it, as they called the process then. I didn't recognize her at first. I thought she was a stranger and cried. But she smiled, and I knew her smile, and was eventually consoled. But her beautiful long dark hair was gone, hair that had never been cut before in her life. Her crown.

There was a pink crêpe-de-chine dress that she wore then that I loved; and, a few years later, a dress of green taffeta shot with gold threads, so that she looked as if she were wearing green leaves shining in the sun. But then we became poor, and any money for clothes went for the children, new shoes or a few yards of broadcloth to make a child's dress.

Red flower, dark eagle.

A real emperor has been in the news. Emperor Hirohito was buried yesterday in Japan. My parents, I fancy, would not have approved tributes to him now. What of those Hong Kong veterans? That's what they would have asked. Or maybe only my father would have asked. He was the one who read newspapers, who talked to soldiers of that war.

Well, the thirties and the forties are buried, or so some people think. (I doubt if any time is ever totally buried.)

I had coffee and crumpets in the James Bay Tea Room today. A small room, crowded with souvenirs of that time, portraits of George VI and Queen Elizabeth, of Churchill in a militant pose; a china bulldog wrapped in a Union Jack; a biscuit tin with marching beefeaters. My father was no royalist, though my mother was, but he admired Churchill. My parents would be familiar with these pictures, these objects, the taste of the strawberry jam. But they were both born in Victoria's time, were young in the days of Edward VII, mature in the time of George V, who was king when I was born. What is quaint to the young waitresses here in the tea shop was glossy with modernity for them. It's what I grew up with. For them, that war was not the first experience of war. They remembered the Boer War and the Great War, the really great war, which ended—and yet did not end—in 1918. "There's a war every twenty years," my father said, as if it were a rule.

I try to remember what my mother said about the first Great War. She had a brother who died in it, and a cousin. My father was in the army. Flour and sugar were scarce, and there were weevils in the flour. Rationing was better managed in the Second War, she thought. War from a housewife's perspective is not the same as from a soldier's. Penelope, keeping the home fires burning and doing her knitting and weaving, does not find war adventurous perhaps, even with suitors on her doorstep, as there so often are during a war.

CARDS: STAR

This card comes later, but I think of it now. This is the beautiful naked lady who pours two urns of water onto the earth. Above her head is a pattern of eight stars, some large, some small. There is an open flower, with a blue butterfly perched on its petals.

My mother had a green thumb. Maybe it was because she was born in April, when the earth is blossoming again after the winter. One of my early memories is of placing seeds in the ground in the place where she told me to put them, and waiting afterwards for flowers to spring up—pansies were they, maybe, or phlox, or marigolds? Even when we lived in town, she planted her rows of beans and peas and potatoes and corn and cucumbers in the backyard. The geraniums and begonias in her kitchen windows were always brilliantly flourishing. But she liked wild flowers too. My sisters and I picked pussywillows for her, and the first violets of spring, and daisies and buttercups and vetch, and even handfuls of dandelions, to be placed in jam jars and admired while the dishes were being washed.

Children were plants too, to be tended and watered. Perhaps also pruned. She hovered over me with special care, her youngest and frailest. She worried, she told me afterwards, that she would not be able to raise me. Children still died more often than they do now. One of my little cousins, at six months. The four-year-old daughter of a neighbour, when I was six or seven.

Sunday, 26 February

This morning I found my way to Christ Church Cathedral, at the corner of Quadra and Courtney. I suppose it's because of my mother that I have the habit of going to some church or other. This one is large, with a damp smell.

Tuesday, 28 February

Where did I intend to take this, if I intended anything? I've been stuck.

DREAM

I am sitting on a bench outside a house where a priest lives. I see a young girl in gingham enter the building and I follow her in my mind into the priest's inner office. She wishes to make a confession, but I don't hear her mention any sin, though she is on her knees. She says to him, "If you were me, would you believe he was faithful?" (Or, "If you were he, would you be faithful?") Afterwards, I see the priest driving the girl in an old-fashioned buggy along a country road. He is a good man, rather elderly, with a broad face.

Dream of a large family gathering. I say to a friend that families ought not to gather more than once a year—it's too uncomfortable. People have nothing in common. It's difficult to share bathrooms.

Later in my dream, I talk to a man who says he dreams in music. He hears in his mind the works of favourite composers. I tell him that I sometimes recite poems in dreams; often poems by Byron, even though he isn't one of my favourite poets. I recite to the man,

"Roll on, thou wide and deep blue ocean, roll."

In the dream, the man and I attend an opera with a French title. I try to translate the title but have difficulties. I keep saying "Struck, struck." The opera is about an animal that is struck. An ass? A donkey?

What is all this about? Is the ass Balaam's ass, or Apuleius' Golden Ass? Or am I saying "Struck" in my dream when I mean "Stuck"? I'm stuck trying to approach my mother, maybe, because I'm being too reasonable, trying to raise her ghost by means of these pictures.

At Christ Church Cathedral on Sunday the Old Testament lesson was of Balaam and his ass. Balaam keeps striking the animal to make it go, but it will not, because there is an angel in the way. In desperation, the faithful animal finally speaks to Balaam, and Balaam sees the angel.

Is where I am going dangerous? Or am I just travelling the wrong road to arrive where I want to?

Is the ass connected with the Golden Ass? In the book by Apuleius, the hero is turned into an ass by a witch. He does not come to his true form again until he encounters the Great Goddess—Isis, is it?—in a procession and kneels to her. He spends the rest of his life in her service.

I should have *The Golden Ass* with me. I should have brought Byron instead of Wordsworth. My mother read Byron when she was a young girl, though her mother forbade her. She too, I think, struggled with her mother. The mother within her. I and my mother am one, to echo a famous text.

Was my mother witch or Isis? Was she both?

Is the girl in gingham myself or my mother? Both? Who is the "he" whose faithfulness is in question? God? My father? All possible lovers? The male Muse? Will the Muse, whether male or female, be faithful to me now?

"Struck" makes me think of the tower struck by lightning. Pride. Non-communication. Solitude. My mother wanted me to be best. Did she inherit that pride from her mother too?

The discomfort of families. Their closeness.

There was a dream—a nightmare—that I used to have for years. It was a dream that someone was smothering me in my bed. Usually I woke up without recognizing the person. Perhaps a fear of rape, I thought. But once I woke knowing that the person who was smothering me in such a close embrace was my mother.

I carry Wordsworth's *Prelude* over to Samuel's Restaurant, where I have lunch. Perhaps I was right to bring it with me, after all. The orphaned Wordsworth sought both mother and father in that capitalized Nature of his. And it was not only beautiful but terrible. The craggy ridges of the mountains rose up and threatened him as he rowed on the moonlit lake. Pain and fear, danger and desire united in his mind. No, he is not just a poet of pretty daffodils.

I too grew up by a lake, near woods and rivers, though not (in spite of our theory that the new world is wilder than the old world) in landscape as harsh and rugged as the Lake District of Wordsworth's childhood might have been. It was lonely enough, though. There were woods where you might have encountered bears and moose. The lake was beautiful, but people drowned in it. My mother would not let me go swimming in it, or skating in winter.

I suppose that's why I thought she smothered me, back then. Because she was so afraid of my hurting myself that she hovered over me, not wanting me to swim or skate. (That's not quite fair, I think. My brothers and sisters swam and skated. We couldn't afford skates for me, by the time I was ready for them. And then we moved.)

Yet whenever my sisters have criticized my mother for being too rigid or severe or puritanical I have argued with them. Yes—there were all those things she disapproved of: alcohol or cards or dancing or divorce. Cakes and ale. But her foot tapped to the music of the dancing. She disobeyed her mother and read Byron. And she had the strength of her rigidity, her incorruptibility. Her faith seemed absolute.

CARDS: THE DEVIL

The devil is an angel and has wings. He is bisexual and has the breasts of a woman.

Is it that I think my mother turned me into a coward? Did she warn me too much against sex, as well as against death by drowning?

My mother, good Baptist that she was by upbringing, had something close to hatred for the Roman Catholic Church, and when I joined it temporarily she was bitter against me. Yet, oddly, I found that I identified her with the church. They both smothered me, I eventually thought. They set up too many rules and commandments. They insisted on being obeyed. They were sure they knew what was good and what was evil.

Could too rigid a virtue be devilish? Is Ayatollah Khomeini's anger against Salman Rushdie motivated by a rigid virtue? Surely that is simply rigidity, not a rigid virtue. I cannot seriously compare my mother to the Ayatollah.

She could not have been totally rigid in her belief, or she would not have joined the Anglican Church to please my father. Who probably did not care.

And if I still go to a church—any church—on Sunday, and re-read *Pilgrim's Progress* and St. Luke's Gospel, I suppose it's because of my mother. I'll probably re-read Byron because of her, too. What was it she liked? *Childe Harold? Manfred?* The lyrics? Not *Don Juan* or any of the other witty poems, I think. They would suit my father better.

1 March

It's a snowy, blizzardy day, the kind of day I came to Victoria to avoid. I haven't walked very far today, only as far as the Bird Cage Confectionery to buy milk and fruit. Now again I sit by my window looking out over Beacon Hill Park. No walkers there this afternoon.

I'm reminded of another blizzardy March day, this time in Sackville, New Brunswick. It's 1962. I've just got off the train at the little station, and see advancing toward me a snow-shrouded figure. The head of the English Department come to meet my train. I've just returned from Bloomington, Indiana, where I had my oral exam for my Ph.D. Safely passed. He congratulates me, takes my suitcase. I ask about my mother, who has been staying in the small Sackville Hospital. "Much the same," he says. They will bring her back home tomorrow. A few days later, her doctor tells me there's no hope for her. But she might as well be home as long as she can. I had guessed, before I took the train to Indiana, that she might be dying, but did not want to know until the trip was over.

The skeleton Death with his scythe. "If I should die before I wake." My mother was 80 when she died, eight years older than her mother had been when she died at 72. Older than her father, who had died in his sixties; older than her brothers, Harry, Murray, George, Charles, Harold and Cecil; older than her sister Grace.

My father died in September, 1959. In the autumn of 1960 my mother moved out to Victoria to live with me. We had a small upstairs apartment in a house in Cook Street: just a kitchen, living-room, bedroom and bath. Really a one-person apartment. I liked it before my mother arrived, when I ate my breakfast in the little kitchen looking out the window at the pear tree down below, and then gathered my books up to take the bus out to Victoria College, where I was teaching in the English Department. I had not done much teaching before, and needed all my time through the week for preparation and marking. But on Saturday morning I would take a bus down town, visit the book shops, relax over a dreamy, peaceful lunch. I felt guilty admitting to myself that my mother spoiled all that. How could I spend every weekday evening marking freshman essays while she knitted in a corner? How could I leave her alone on Saturday when I was the only person in town she knew? How could I sleep and share a room with my mother, who had never slept alone in her life until my father died? It was a dreadful year. For both of us, probably.

Sackville, where we moved in the fall of 1961, was somewhat better. I was working in the Mount Allison Library instead of teaching, and was freer in the evening. Again we were in an upstairs apartment, but it was slightly bigger. There were friendly neighbours. The landlord and landlady were kind.

But shortly after Christmas my mother took sick. At first it was just that she was lame. What was making her lame? Her foot was swollen and covered with sores. It was a circulatory disorder. She would probably have to have the foot amputated. But she could not stand the thought of an amputation. The pills she took for the pain gave her hallucinations, destroyed her memory.

No, it's too painful. I'm stuck. I can't go on, unless I flog my mind, as Balaam flogged his patient beast of burden.

From January to May is a short illness by some standards. By others it's long.

The bedroom was a large room with two single beds. When my mother said that terrifying little elves—evil, dirty creatures—were getting into bed with her and teasing her, I got her to trade with me. For a night or so, it worked, but the creatures pursued her, she said, to the other bed. There was a hide-a-bed in the living-room which I made up and tried to sleep in when I was desperate for rest. That bed was big enough for both of us; she followed me into it and held my hand all night to protect her against the elves and demons. I lay awake with a transistor radio at my head, listening to whatever music was on—Elvis? the Beatles?—in order to keep my own sanity. At some point during the night I burst into silent tears. I had thought my mother was asleep, but she touched my wet cheek and said, wonderingly, "You're crying. Why?"

Later, my sister Marion came to be with us. Later still, shortly before she died, my mother entered the hospital again. It was a bizarre touch that in Sackville at that time the undertaker's hearse doubled as the ambulance. I don't wonder there was panic in her eyes when she was lifted in. "She knows she'll never come out," Marion said to me later.

When I visited her in the hospital, she introduced me to the woman in the next bed. "Mrs. Estey," she said, "this is my mother."

Mrs. Estey and I exchanged smiles.

She had told me once that she didn't much like her mother. But she did love her.

The angel with the trumpet blows for resurrection day. The dead arise from their tombs.

Who am I to judge my mother? I loved her.

"If religion weren't true, life would all have been wasted," she said to me once, not long before she was taken to the hospital. "It wouldn't have been worth living."

"Surely not," I said, for—whether religion is true or not—life is a good. My mother had had a husband who loved her; she had had children; she had had friends; she had grown geraniums in the kitchen window. She had defied her mother and read Byron. It was her pain that spoke through her, not her true self.

She is the Strong Woman who has overcome the lion. She is the dancer of the final card, the card of consummation, who dances framed in a wreath of everlasting green.

I have not lately dreamed the dream of being smothered, by my mother or anyone else. Sometimes I dream of moving into a new house with my mother and father and others now dead. We unpack the books and the dishes. Outside the window is an old-fashioned rose garden, and the fragrance of the roses blows all through the house. Or perhaps it is a wild apple tree, or a lilac bush. The new moon rises, and the fool and his little dog dance in its light. Maybe death and the devil will dance, too. And the angel, the eagle, the ox and the lion who stand at the four corners of my bed and protect it from harm.

2 March

Sunshine on the snow. A blue sky like the sky over the prairies.

DREAM:

I am reading a novel in which there are three central characters, Sylvia, Hugh and James. The novel is written in three parts, from the point of view of each of the characters. Is one of the men Sylvia's father or husband? The other is more detached, an objective commentator. Who is Sylvia? Hugh is Sylvia? Is Sylvia Hugh? Does Sylvia contain all three? Is Sylvia my mother? Am I Sylvia?

Long ago, when I was a student at university, I had a dream of a young man who had the disconcerting habit of turning into his mother. His life was ruined. Young, brilliant, ambitious, he wished to enter public life, to attain a commanding position. But, just as he was about to make a speech or assume authority, his mother would take over. He would disappear, her skirts would sweep the ground. The voice and the words would be hers.

Did I object to being a woman? Or did I simply fear that I was overwhelmed by the power of my mother's personality? Swallowed up in her?

I thought then that the dream was a nightmare. Now I can see that there are worse things than being taken over—temporarily—by my mother's ghost. She speaks from my depths. But the others are in me too: the cool observer, the Muse who is husband and father, the voice of Athena's owl, crying out, "Who, who?"

GREAT-AUNT REBECCA

I remember my mother's Aunt Rebecca
who remembered very well Confederation
and what a time of mourning it was.
She remembered the days before the railway,
and how when the first train came through
everybody got on and visited it,
scraping off their shoes first
so as not to dirty the carriage.
She remembered the remoteness, the long walks between
    neighbours.
Her own mother had died young, in childbirth,
but she had lived till her eighties,
had borne eleven children,
managed to raise nine of them,
in spite of scarlet fever.
She had clothed them with the work of her own fingers,
wool from her own sheep, spun at home,
woven at home, sewed at home
without benefit of machine.
She had fed them with pancakes and salt pork
and cakes sweetened with maple sugar.
She had taught them one by one to memorize
"The chief end of man is to know God,"
and she had also taught them to make porridge
and the right way of lighting a wood fire,
had told the boys to be kind and courageous
and the girls never to raise their voices
or argue with their husbands.

I remember her as an old woman,
rheumatic, with folded hands,
in a rocking-chair in a corner of the living-room,
bullied (for her own good) by one of her daughters.

She marvelled a little, gently and politely,
at radios, cars, telephones;
but really they were not as present to her
as the world of her prime, the farmhouse
in the midst of the woods, the hayfields
where her husband and the boys swung their scythes
through the burning afternoon, until she called for supper.

For me also, the visiting child, she made that world more
    real
than the present could be. I too
wished to be a pioneer,
to walk on snowshoes through remote pastures,
to live away from settlements an independent life
with a few loved people only; to be like Aunt Rebecca,
soft as silk and tough as that thin wire
they use for snaring rabbits.

Visit of Condolence

Ruth was standing at the front door of the trailer, leaning on her crutches when they drove up. She had expected them, of course, though she hadn't been quite sure what time of day they would arrive. It was in fact around one o'clock. She raised one hand from a crutch and waved at them as they got out of the car, Clemmie's blue Chevvy. That was Clemmie, Steve's niece, driving, and Clemmie's mother, Edith, was sitting beside her. Then they had to push the seat forward and let out the other sisters from the back seat. Thelma and Anna. They clustered in a little group, Steve's three sisters, with Clemmie to one side, as if she were a guide maybe, someone necesary who doesn't quite belong. It was the first time Anna had visited since Steve's death. She lived out west and hadn't been able to get to the funeral. The others had been over for the funeral, but only Thelma, who lived nearby, had visited since. Of course Ruth herself hadn't been here at the trailer until this week. With her broken leg in a cast, she hadn't been able to do for herself, and she had spent her time with one or the other of her sisters.

Edith was the only one of the sisters wearing slacks. She had also put on a red blouse, as if she were trying to cheer herself up. Although she was over 70, her figure was still youthful, though her hair was totally white. Thelma, Ruth thought, looked older than Edith. Her face was wrinkled and leathery, under tight, sausage-like curls. Both she and Anna—the baby of the family at 60—wore summer skirts and blouses. Anna was the only one who still had some dark in her hair, though it was streaked with grey.

"Come in, come in," Ruth said, opening the door, half-embracing each of them as they entered. Rather a pretty woman, Anna thought, with her wavy white hair and soft brown eyes. Close to Anna's age. She led the way into the interior of the trailer, which was larger and more comfortable than Anna had expected. Anna's only experience with trailers had been of the kind that could actually go on a journey. This was a real little house. Ruth and Steve had moved into it the previous fall, when Steve had no longer been able to manage the stairs and the furnace at the farmhouse, Ruth's old home, where they had lived the first ten years of their marriage. They had lived then with Ruth's mother, who had died not long after they moved out, at the age of 90.

"Did you have a good trip?" Ruth asked. "When did you start out? Do any of you need to go to the bathroom?"

Edith needed to go. That bottle of pop she had drunk in order to take her pills. Anna followed her later, looking around curiously to see the rest of the trailer. There was a living-room, a large kitchen with a round table, a bedroom, which Anna only glimpsed, the bathroom. She peered out the bathroom window at the yard, where grass was growing high. Masses of daisies, buttercups, raggedy clover, timothy. There was a clothesline—it must be the clothesline where Ruth was hanging the clothes the morning in April, after a late snow-storm, when she slipped and broke her leg.

Back to the living-room, where they all sat around deco-rously, Ruth in the big, overstuffed chair that had been Steve's favourite ("I have to sit here because of the crutches," she said apologetically), Clemmie in a hard chair near the door, Edith near her on the tall chair carved with vines and leaves, Thelma and Anna on the chesterfield with their backs to the window. Even Thelma, who usually talked all the time, seemed for the moment to find it hard to scrape up something to say. It was up to Anna, the one who had not attended the funeral, to inquire about the state of Ruth's health, to say, "You've cer-tainly had a hard time since my last visit. Your mother. Stevie. Everything."

"Yes indeed, yes indeed," Ruth sighed. "And we had such a nice visit with you last summer."

"And Stevie seemed so well, too."

"Yes. Not that he really was altogether. He was already having some trouble with his breathing."

Anna remembered last summer's visit. She had spent two nights at the farmhouse. Late-night supper around the kitchen table, she and Ruth and Stevie. What had they eaten? French fries? Hamburgers? Doughnuts? Pie? Stevie had rolled his own cigarettes, as usual. A stocky figure, pepper-and-salt hair, protruding blue eyes, thick hands with one fin-ger of one hand cut off at the knuckle. In the war? In the woods? In a trucking accident? She must've known once but had forgotten.

"It was his heart finally, was it?" she asked.

"Well, he had the heart, of course. But it was mainly his breathing. Emphysema. He thought the cancer had come

74

back on him, that bowel thing, but the doctor told me it hadn't, it was the pain from his breathing. He just kept refusing to go to the doctor. Then it all came to a head when I fell and broke my leg. He would insist on coming up to the hospital in the ambulance with me. It was too much for him. He took sick that night and phoned my brother Howie. Howie started off to Fredericton with him, but he died on the way."

Anna had heard this before, over the telephone. "He was lucky in a way," Thelma said. "He might have died 40 years ago, with the cancer." Young Stevie, then, with another wife, Pearl. Long phone reports to the parents from Pearl in northern Ontario. Anna was living at home then, working at a lawyer's office in Fredericton. What a lot of worry Stevie had caused them at one time or another. Pearl and the war and everything.

"Your mother too," Anna said. "Of course she had reached an age..."

Quite a lively old lady, in fact. Stevie thought her difficult. Maybe Ruth was too devoted to her, Anna wondered.

"Aren't any of you ladies hungry?" Clemmie asked. "What about that lunch we brought?"

"Oh, you brought your own lunch?" Ruth said, looking faintly relieved. "I had mine before you came. I had no idea when you'd be here, and I'm not able to get around much to cook. I thought maybe we'd eat at the restaurant in town."

"You said that on the phone," Anna said, "but we decided we'd rather make our own. I'm starved, Clemmie."

They had had a great discussion the night before at Clemmie's place, when they were eating dinner. Should they make sandwiches? No, they would just buy the *fixin's,* as the old people would've said. And, before they left Fredericton in the morning, they had stopped and bought brown bread, cold meatloaf, cold ham, butter, cheese, tomatoes, bananas, plums, strawberries. Clemmie had a hamper with ice to keep the stuff cool. It really made quite a spread, piled up on Ruth's kitchen table.

In the kitchen, a sort of subdued hilarity came over them, at least over Anna and Clemmie and Thelma. Clemmie made the coffee, buttered the bread and passed around hunks of meat and cheese. She perched on the kitchen stool to eat. There were chairs enough for the others, although they were rather squeezed around the table. Ruth had put out some of her crabapple pickles, her mother's recipe. "Delicious." Anna said.

Anna was reminded of the day after her mother's funeral, twenty years ago. She and Edith and Stevie and Stevie's young son Walter—Pearl's son—were all sitting together at Uncle Bert's kitchen table eating potato salad and baked beans dished up for them by Uncle Bert's wife, Aunt Mabel. It was late May; there was an apple tree in blossom in the yard. She had been terribly, indecently hungry, and half-amused by Stevie's jokes, though she was also half-crying. Stevie and Walter took turns driving the car back to Fredericton that afternoon. They were speeding, especially when Walter was driving. Anna and Edith had both been frightened. And then—her mind dived again—there was that time when Grandma had been dead in the coffin at Uncle Ted's and she (only nine years old then) had sat with her mother and all the aunts and uncles in Uncle Ted's little closed-in parlour. The smell of foxes, which a neighbour across the road kept, had drifted in through the open window, and Anna had wondered if it could be Grandma smelling already. Her mother half-horrified, half-amused, when she asked her later. Must've been around this time of year, late June or early July. She and Edith and Thelma had been picking strawberries to earn money. Mother, after going home, had dyed all her clothes black. The dye bubbling on the stove had smelled funny too. Death and dyeing. Silly joke. Mother and Grandmother would've remembered other deaths, wakes, funeral parties.

"No, Walter didn't make it to the funeral," Ruth was saying. "He was in California. It was too far for him. Philip was here from Kingston, of course."

"Yes, I heard that." Philip, the younger son, the favourite, the good boy. Pearl's son, too, but young enough when his father married Ruth so that a bond had been established. Hope he'll keep in touch with her. Easy enough for blood bonds to slide away, let alone these frailer relationships. Poor boy. He's had a bad year too. Pearl last fall and now Stevie, his mother and father both in one year's time. Mustn't mention Pearl to Ruth, of course. Not tactful. Though tact was something she had never claimed for herself.

It was Thelma, Ruth, Anna who talked now. Clemmie said little, though she waited on the others, asked questions sometimes. Edith said nothing, brooded in her chair. Maybe I shouldn't have urged her to come, Thelma and Anna each thought separately, their thoughts meeting. in mid-air. She had certainly not wanted to come.

However, here they were now, at Ruth's place, and Edith was not saying anything, though she ate her lunch with a good enough appetite. Of course Edith was nearest Stevie's age. She was 70, he had been 72. They had been toddlers together. She must have all sorts of memories, Anna thought. And it was a warning. Death must seem to be breathing down her neck. Down all their necks.

After the strawberries, they moved again into the living-room. "I'll wash the dishes," Clemmie said. Not that there were many, just the cups and saucers and the fruit nappies, because they had eaten their sandwiches from paper plates. "I'll help you," Edith said, but Clemmie shook her head and pushed her mother into the room with the others.

"I've been dying for a smoke, Ruth," Edith finally broke her silence. "Do you mind?"

"Oh, of course not, Edith. There's one of Steve's ashtrays, right behind you."

It gave her a turn. Stevie's ashtray. But she took it—it was a big brown pottery affair—and lit her cigarette anyway. Of course you could be sure Ruth wouldn't smoke, she was such a goody-goody. Anna didn't, either. Pearl had, of course. Thelma smoked sometimes, and she did now. "I'll keep you company," she said. Being tactful? Maybe she needed it too, you never knew.

"I see you have one of those scenic clocks, Ruth," Thelma said. "Tilly gave me one of them for my birthday, but I like yours better. You don't notice the clock so much. You'd just think it was a picture."

"Yes—Steve bought it for me for Christmas. He thought that house was like one you lived in when you were growing up."

"The Old Orchard house. That's what it's like. Do you remember, Edith?" Thelma asked.

"Yes. Well, maybe." She was peering at it dubiously.

"Before my time, the Orchard house," Anna said.

"That's where Stevie pushed me out the upstairs window," Edith said. "Little devil. Nearly broke my neck. Stevie was always a card."

Anna laughed. "Happy childhood memories," she said. "Thank goodness he was more grownup before I came along."

"I was the one who got you up on the roof, remember, Anna?" Thelma said. "And you wouldn't come down until Dad came with a ladder. Got me into a lot of trouble, you did."

There were several photos on the walls: Stevie with a horse, smiling into the camera; Stevie with one of the big trucks he used to drive before he retired; Stevie and Ruth on their wedding day, a mature bride and groom—she in her fifties, he in his sixties. Whatever had happened to those earlier wedding pictures, Stevie and Pearl? Must look in my old trunks and boxes, Edith thought. I might still have one. Not likely Ruth even saw them. Bet she'd be curious. Stevie in uniform then. Pearl holding tight to his arm. Already pregnant with Walter, but luckily she didn't show.

"Would you like to see the funeral book with the list of people who called?" Ruth asked. "There are lots of names. Steve was very popular."

She sat between Thelma and Anna on the sofa, turning the pages of the book. Thelma knew most of these names, Anna few, familiar in childhood, but not connected in her mind with grownup people. "I won't look," Edith said. "I already know about them."

("It was too big a funeral," Edith had told Anna. "I don't want a big funeral like that. Have me cremated and stored in the kitchen cupboard, or give my body to medical science."

"Don't tell me, tell Clemmie," Anna had said. "I'm not your next of kin."

"Pearl was cremated. She wanted to be cremated, Philip told me."

"Did she give her body to medical science?"

"No—maybe she didn't think of it. She probably didn't think she'd die so suddenly."

"Death's always sudden," Anna had said sententiously, and knew she sounded like their mother.)

Clemmie had finished the dishes and now came into the room.

"Is that Uncle Steve with the horse?" she asked. "My, he looks young there. Who are that couple with the kids?"

"That's Philip and Fay and their little ones," Ruth said. "Doesn't the little boy look like your Uncle Steve? Would you like to look at my photograph album?"

She dislodged the album from under the Bible. Edith came over and looked at these snapshots too. More photos of Stevie. She had one of his early army photos, from back there when he was married to Pearl. But of course no Pearl. The missing snapshots were sliding before Edith's eyes, before Anna's eyes. Pearl with Stevie and little Walter. Pearl and her three sisters-in-law. Pearl and Stevie and Edith and Ross, both men in uniform. Pearl alone, dressed for some sort of masquerade as if she were a chorus girl. Pearl with black hair, brown eyes darker than Ruth's, red lips. Pearl pouting and strutting. Pearl later on, beginning to lose her looks, begining to look tired and frayed, but still vital. Were there ghosts, Anna wondered? If there were, would Pearl or Stevie be the ones most likely to haunt?

79

There were snapshots of Ruth, too. Ruth and Stevie. Ruth and her brothers and sisters. Ruth and her parents.

"Oh, you have some really old ones," Anna exclaimed. "Who's the man with the beard and all those girls in long dresses?"

"That's my grandfather and grandmother. Those are all my aunts, my father's sisters. Aunt Elsie died young. That's my father at the far left. And a friend of my father's."

The friend was a young woman leaning close to the young man, Ruth's father. She looked handsome and in high spirits. Another of those ghosts?

"Now I don't know if you'll want to look at these," Ruth said, taking out an envelope. "Some people don't, but my sisters wanted them taken. It's my mother in her casket."

Edith looked away. So did Clemmie. "Gross," she thought, using her daughter Dilys' word. "Morbid."

But Anna, in spite of a shiver of revulsion, looked them through deliberately before handing them to Thelma. Always look at everything, within reason, she thought. This doll-like mannequin in the coffin really bore little resemblance to the perky old lady she had talked to last summer. But thank goodness Ruth hadn't done this for (to?) Stevie. The luxury of grief. Though why not, if it really made you feel better?

"Do you want to visit any of the relatives while you're here? Cousins or aunts?" Clemmie asked. "I think the sun's come out."

"I can't think of anyone, Clemmie," Edith said. "I've lost touch with them all. Maybe Anna wants to see someone."

"What about the graveyard?" Anna asked. "Since I wasn't here for the funeral." Might as well get it over with, she thought.

"Yes, of course," Ruth said. "I'll go along with you. I'd like the chance."

Edith made a face. Whatever possessed Anna to suggest going to the graveyard? How could Anna and Thelma and Ruth look so calmly at the pictures of that old woman in her

coffin? They would all be in the graveyard soon enough themselves, forever and a day. She didn't want to go with them now,
but she couldn't very well say so.

Clemmie knew she had a problem. Her mother couldn't
stand the back seat; she said it always made her sick. Luckily,
Aunt Thelma and Aunt Anna had seemed to be comfortable
enough there on the drive over. It had given Aunt Thelma a
chance to point out the old landmarks to Aunt Anna. But of
course this time Ruth, with her crutches, had to be in front.
"You'll have to sit in the back with us, Edith," Thelma said.
"It's just a short drive."

So there they were, all three of them, wedged in side by
side, like three peas in a pod, bursting the pod. Really, Edith
thought she would choke.

The drive from the trailer to the graveyard was only a short
one. Ruth directed Clemmie, who did not know the way. It
was Clemmie who had to help the women out of the car. All
except Edith, who had decided to stay in the car. "You folks go
and look at graves," she said. "I'm not getting out."

"I'm having grass put on," Ruth said. "The Legion said
they'd provide a stone; but if I don't like it when I see it I can
always put up a different one."

"Yes, of course." Thelma said.

Stevie had hated the army, Anna thought. And he had had
a military funeral. Was that only just and fair, or one of those
dumb jokes death plays on people? He had not been one to
plan his own funeral. "One thing for sure, they can't leave you
on the surface," he had said once when he had been talking to
Edith and Anna.

It was like Anna, Thelma thought, to wander off looking at
other tombstones instead of staying by Stevie's grave. There
she was, wandering away over the graveyard toward that line
of evergreens, bending now and then to look at names on the
stones. She said she had arthritis, but it didn't seem to affect
her walking at all. Thelma herself continued to stand by the
grave, talking in a low, consoling voice to Ruth and Clemmie.

This was a lonely graveyard, she thought. Not like the one where Fred and her little boy, Georgie, were buried. That was right next to the church, St. Michael's Church, where she could visit now and then after service. She wouldn't want to be buried in this place. But she wouldn't say that to Ruth, of course.

"The motorcyclists drive through here at a great clip sometimes," Ruth said. "They use it as a place for racing in. Seems disgraceful."

Thelma shook her head and sighed sympathetically. Not that Stevie would mind, supposing he knew about it. He had been a lively one himself when he felt like it. Speeding through a graveyard, tossing a bottle out on a grave, that was something she could imagine Stevie doing. "Give those old bones something to revive them," he might have said.

Remember that old Depression song they used to sing, taking off the hymn?

Hallelujah give us a handout
and revive us again.

Stevie used to sing that. Grandma didn't like him to sing songs like that. Or Mama either, for that matter.

Anna, wandering among the tombstones, looked up and saw that the sky was almost totally clear now. A few white clouds drifting harmlessly in the sky. Smell of clover. Ankle-thick grass. Buttercups. She stopped to watch a bee, which was moving from clover blossom to clover blossom, making each head dip down while it milked it—honeyed it?—and then moved on elsewhere. The flowers popped up, lighter. So much life in graveyards. And all these people whose names she knew. It was like a little village, with uncles, aunts, cousins, old neighbours. Uncle Bert and Aunt Mabel. Uncle Ted. Why, he was just 60 when he died. My age. I thought he was so old, back then. Of course Pearl isn't buried in this graveyard. Probably buried in Texas. Must get back. Clemmie won't want to stay much longer.

It was all very well for Thelma and Anna, Edith thought, watching them from the car. They'd been so much younger than Stevie, they hardly knew him. Though now Thelma went around saying how close he'd been to her. Just because she lived nearer to him in the last years. That story she'd been telling the other night about how he'd brought her up to the trailer to visit a few weeks before he died when Ruth had to be with her mother, how he'd stayed up all night talking to her, telling her about his army days, all that out of his past. She herself was the one he'd been close to. Why hadn't he come and brought her home with him, stayed up talking to her all night? And Ruth—Ruth was an outsider. Nice enough, but they'd only been married for ten—no, eleven—years. If it had been Pearl, they could've got drunk together at the kitchen table and cried.

There now—there was Anna coming back; she and Thelma and Clemmie all gathered around Ruth. They were coming back to the car, Ruth on her crutches.

Thelma, helping to support Ruth, suddenly had one of those chills you have at times, even on warm days. "Somebody's walking on my grave," as they used to say when they were children. She caught herself in time before she said it aloud.

After they had driven Ruth back home from the graveyard and seen her into the trailer, there didn't seem to be much reason for staying. "I need to get home," Clemmie said. "The kids'll be expecting me." (Not that they'd worry too much, she thought.)

"Of course," Ruth said. "I know how it is. It would've been nice to have had a longer visit, but another time."

She stood at the door, leaning on a crutch with one arm, waving goodbye with the other arm. The smile on her face was fixed.

She would have to get supper for herself. They had left the

meat and the plums. Might as well eat something. Make herself a cup of tea. And now that Steve's sisters were gone, she could have a good cry. "Steve," she wanted to say aloud, but didn't, "I miss you." There was no answer. She knew he had been mourning Pearl. But he hadn't wanted to say. What could she have said to him?

Clemmie was driving the same route back, but faster.

"Maybe you enjoyed that visit," Edith said, "but I didn't enjoy it at all."

"Enjoy? You weren't supposed to enjoy," Thelma said. "We were visiting Ruth for Stevie's sake, and maybe to make her feel better."

"But—but—but," Edith said, and she began to blubber, as she had when she and Stevie were children, "Stevie never did anything he didn't enjoy, did he?"

Of course he did, Anna thought, but didn't say. We all do. "Let's all have dinner together at the hotel when we get back," she said. "They have a decent buffet. We can get a table looking out on the river. Maybe you'd enjoy that."

FOR MY BROTHER

Brother, I seldom wrote you letters,
you wrote me none
that I recall,
except maybe a line or so
scrawled at the end
of Christmas notes from wives or girlfriends.

Now, what's the postal code
for that plot of ground in the cemetery
where you are resting next my parents,
who sometimes grumbled when they were alive
that you never visited them except to borrow money?
Yet they loved you,
you loved them.

And I?

It's a matter of blood and seed,
the tangling of veins and roots.
You can call it love
or maybe necessity
kinship not always kind.

Somewhere at the back of my eyes
I see us together in the nineteen-thirties,
you on your bicycle,
me riding the handlebars
down a soft gravel road
between lines of trees
and dandelions in ditches.

There at the back of my eyes
you will always be young, and I

your little sister in a cotton dress
and ribbed cotton stockings. Is that
what's meant by immortality?

You died the day before Easter. Now it's May,
after the spring snows. Dandelions
come out on my lawn, which you never saw.
I'm determined not to kill them
with weed-killer, as the neighbours do,
but pick the flowers and bring them
into the kitchen to put in jam jars
as we did for our mother when we were children
these sturdy vinous flowers with edible leaves,
these multiple rays of sunlight

they will shine forever

Essence of Marigold

I am sitting here at my dining-room table staring at a large yellow marigold that I bought this morning in the Farmers' Market. Only ten cents, but beautiful and crinkly, undeniably real. Marigolds have almost no scent, it's true, but if I press my nose right up against it, this one gives off a faint spicy odour, like some kind of kitchen herb. Not at all sweet, mildly medicinal in fact, but pleasant. I have put it in a little brown pottery vase and set it in the centre of the table. Geraniums also: a double red geranium in a tin container. Exactly the shade of red geranium my mother would have liked.

Should I paint one of them? A still life, say—marigold and transistor radio? Geranium on window-sill, with prairie city beyond it? (The geranium must stay in the tin container, which must not be camouflaged in any way.) No. I don't feel like painting them. I have painted flowers from time to time (pale narcissi in a brown pot set against a blue background; also those deep red, semi-purplish gladioli now framed on my living-room wall). I think I was trying to hold on to them, but these flowers I intend to let go. I couldn't catch their scent, anyway. (The geranium, some people would say, has no scent. Except in the leaves.) And anyhow I have gone on to other things than flowers. Prairie landscapes. Crowd scenes. I am a good painter. Maybe not great, but good. Too conscientious, maybe? Not experimental enough? A failure in imagination? My fans (and I have fans, bless them) wouldn't say so. They think of me as a female prairie Alex Colville—or maybe that Alex Colville is a male Maritime Daisy Lister. If I don't have quite Colville's reputation, I have the excuse that I'm a few years younger.

I'm a few years younger than Marguerite Chrystal, too. An admirable painter, though unlike Alex Colville. The magic without the realism. If she painted the marigold, she would paint its essence. One might think of the heart of the sun, or of the ruffled flight of a ballerina. (I have a fleeting image of a ballerina as I might paint her: I would concentrate, I think, on the muscles. Ballerinas are really tough ladies. I like that combination of toughness and grace.)

Marguerite is in my mind just now because she has painted my portrait. Oh, not in oils. No, she has written a short story about me. (Marguerite, unfairly, has several talents.) She told me about this story, said she would send me a copy, but forgot to. I ran across it yesterday in the public library, stood reading it at the magazine rack, trying to decide in my mind whether I liked it, as the ballet dancer might stand in front of my portrait of her, objecting to the prominence of her muscles. Has she caught my essence, I wonder?

88

Really, though, the story is not so much about me as it is about memory. Here are two women, two painters, who have quite different memories of the occasion when they met. Which is telling the truth? Are there two truths?

I have a diary dating from the time I met Marguerite. I have a bundle of letters from her. (She has forgotten she wrote me.) I have clippings about exhibitions, a few sketches. I could look them up, I could document this account, but I don't intend to this time. I'll try to get at the essence.

I arrived in Saskatoon by myself on the train that day, the day I was to collect the prize. (I insist that I arrived by myself, although Marguerite is equally certain that my parents came with me.) My certainty springs from the fact that my arrival by myself was a triumph. I was my parents' only child and too much protected. I had never been separated from my mother for more than a day. On this occasion, however, I had argued (successfully) that I was perfectly able to look after myself. After all, I was almost seventeen. (Marguerite remembers me as younger, a plump, composed child, perhaps twelve, four-teen at most. I was, in fact, rather thin, if not scrawny, and not at all composed.) The trip to Saskatoon from Kasoba was not a difficult one, although rather long, and I was to be met at the railway station by one of the local artists, a Mrs. Curtis, who was putting me up in her house. Lucky that Mrs. Curtis made that offer. If I had been staying at an hotel, for instance, my parents would not have felt I should be alone. But they could not have afforded a good hotel, either for themselves or for me. Once before, I had won a prize for a watercolour, but had not been able to come. If I had I'd have spent all my prize money.

Now, as the train chugged its way through the autumn fields, stopping here and there at small prairie towns, I was torn between delight and fear. I was free, and I was about to encounter the unknown. I ate the egg sandwiches and solid doughnuts that my mother had packed for my lunch, half in a delightful daydream, half in nervous fear that something would go wrong.

Saskatoon station. Much larger than the station at Kasoba, and I have never been here before. I am wearing a navy-blue suit, handed down to me by a cousin in Ontario who is a year or so older than I am. I hate it, but am lucky to have it. Anyhow, I have told Mrs. Curtis that I will be wearing this navy-blue suit. I have no idea what she will be wearing or what she will look like. For some reason I imagine her with white hair, fat like the eldest of my aunts.

While I stand there uncertainly, there rushes up to me a trim little woman in a smart dress—I can't describe it, I just know it is smart—with her coat flung over her shoulders. Her hair is piled up on top of her head in an auburn mass, from which a few wisps have escaped. She is holding a chubby little boy, three or four years old, by the hand. They look as if they have both been running.

"Daisy Lister?" she gasps. "I'm Bea Curtis."

Mrs. Curtis takes charge of me immediately. I am whisked, with my little battered suitcase (my mother's little battered suitcase, that is) out of the station and into a taxi. Taxis are rather outside the range of my experience. In Kasoba everything is within walking distance. I walk to school every day; my father walks to the drugstore where he works for his small wartime salary; my parents and I walk to church together on Sunday. Sometimes one of my uncles who is better off than my father takes us for a drive in his car, but not too often. Mrs. Curtis and the little boy (Binker, he is called) and I all sit together in the back seat of the taxi. I am delighted with Saskatoon. It has trees and a river, as Kasoba hasn't, and a huge hotel that looks like a castle. "Pretty river," Mrs. Curtis says abstractedly to Binker.

I think that she is speaking to me, and say "Yes" a little too fervently. She looks at me with surprise, and I turn a bright pink (I feel the blood rushing into my face) and lapse into silence.

I am to collect the prize for my watercolour that evening, at a meeting of the Group. The Group is trying to encourage talent in improbable places like Kasoba. That is why I am here. It is Marguerite who has written to me before, and I rather wish I could have stayed with her, but she does not have room. She is a genuine artist (I suspect that Mrs. Curtis isn't) and is living in some hand-to-mouth artistic way in a single room.

Mrs. Curtis settles me into a trim little room in her trim little house. She looks me over thoughtfully. There is time, she thinks, to put a few pin curls in my hair. What do I plan to wear? I have a new dress, bought especially for the occasion, a green flowered dress with a fussy lace collar. I like it myself, and in Kasoba it seemed right, but I see through Mrs. Curtis' eyes that it is all wrong. Perhaps without the lace? It was the lace that I had especially liked, but Mrs. Curtis persuades me (tactfully, tactfully) to allow her to take the collar off while I am having a nap before dinner. Not that I do have a nap before dinner. (Supper, we called it in Kasoba.)

At dinner, I meet Mr. Curtis, who is a business man in the city, rather older than Mrs. Curtis and beginning to go bald. He is a friendly man. "I like your painting, Daisy," he says. "I don't know much about art—Bea's the artist around here—but I thought you should get the prize. That field of black-eyed Susans—I do like that."

I see that his opinion isn't to be taken seriously, but he is kind. I like him, as I like Mrs. Curtis. I am intimidated, however, by the fact that there is a maid who waits on the table and even wears a uniform. Nobody that I know in Kasoba has a maid. I find it difficult to talk in the presence of somebody who is in the room but not part of the company. Anyhow, it is hard for me to keep my mind on dinner or on Mr. and Mrs. Curtis. I am thinking of the evening to come, of meeting Marguerite, of being presented with my prize.

The meeting that night is in an artist's studio (Marguerite and I agree on that). A big attic room without much furniture;

91

burlap curtains at the windows; canvases propped against walls. There are some poets present as well as the painters. (I remember a dentist who told me he wrote a sonnet a day and kept his writings in a barrel.) Marguerite has not yet arrived when Mrs. Curtis and I come in. The studio is like a stage waiting for its leading lady. (Though surely I am the leading lady for that evening, the Promising Young Artist from out there in Kasoba?) There is a handsome young man present with dark hair and brown eyes who seems to me the leading man and who attaches himself to Marguerite as soon as she comes in.

2

It is morning again (Sunday morning), and I look once more at my marigold and the geranium, which have survived the night very well. The marigold has perceptibly more scent today than yesterday. A scent like that of the marigolds in my mother's garden, although hers were the tiny button marigolds rather than large ones like this. There was a thunderstorm last night—one of those thorough-going prairie storms—and the sky is still sullen: but patches of blue show through the clouds, and I hear crows cawing. I drink a cup of coffee and read over what I have written. Why, I wonder, do I delay so long about actually bringing Marguerite onto the scene? Is it because I am afraid I can't possibly paint her essence? Her essence has always seemed to me a mystery, untouchable. I, on the other hand, am not at all mysterious. I have often painted my own portrait, not so much from any great narcissism as from the realization that I look like so many other people I know. My mother told me early on, "You may be talented, but that doesn't make you better than other people." I tend to agree with her: painters, poets, millionaires may have some special ability to handle paints or words or money, but we are really only ordinary people with one highly developed skill, like jugglers or *cordon bleu* chefs.

Neverthless, I didn't think Marguerite was ordinary. I didn't expect her to be ordinary. There was something extraordinary about her letters, even their appearance on the page. Her handwriting was excited and angular, with high loops that reminded me of bird-wings, quite unlike my own careful schoolgirlish hand. Her sentences were breathless, flying in all directions at once. On the margins there were often quick sketches of creatures on the wing, fabulous birds, butterflies, sometimes weirdly distorted and frightening, but always strangely beautiful.

When I imagined her—created an image of her to go with the letters—I imagined someone small and quick and bird-like, with piercing bright eyes. I saw her in my mind dancing in bare feet with peacock plumes in her hair. The real Marguerite wasn't like that. She was handsome, though—handsome rather than beautiful, I think—a tall, statuesque young woman somewhere in her twenties. She was dark (there I had guessed right) and glowed rather, I fancied, like those spikes of crimson gladioli that I painted later with their purple shadows. I was—and yet was not—disappointed, and stood there readjusting my vision of her while she bent over me (she was so much taller than I). I caught a surprised expression also on her face. "You don't look the way I imagined you," she said, but did not elaborate, and I fanced that she must be disappointed, that she had possibly invented someone more flower-like as the painter of those black-eyed Susans and red lilies. Years later, she told me, "It was your age. I hadn't expected someone quite so young, a mere child."

"I wasn't a mere child," I said indignantly, remembering my seventeen years, from which she had so absurdly subtracted. (At that point she remembered me as having been only ten. She almost fancied having met me with a doll in my arms.)

Still, I suppose I did seem younger than my age. My parents had babied me, and I was a shy little person without many friends. I had not yet been out with a boy. Even for Kasoba, I guess I was backward. There is some truth, then, in her memory of me as being a mere child. A partial truth.

As far as the presentation with the prize is concerned, I don't remember it at all. I suppose the prize was a cheque. I went home afterwards with money, which I spent rather foolishly in my mother's opinion. (I also sold the painting of the black-eyed Susans to Mr. Curtis, who wanted it for his office. My first sale.) I don't remember who handed me the prize. Marguerite, maybe? Mrs. Curtis? Some man or other, more likely. I envisage someone older and dimmer. Marguerite remembers me as very composed at the time of the presentation, pleased but unimpressed. Possibly. She also has distinct memories of both my parents and of their reactions. Quite untrue, of course. My parents were not there. As I keep insisting.

After the presentation, the meeting turned into a party. There were drinks, cocktails possibly, beer possibly. I think I had a ginger ale. My parents, I knew, would not have approved my drinking anything stronger. Perhaps indeed ginger ale was all I was offered.

I sat, I remember, next to Marguerite and the dark young man. I don't remember his name, but I fancy (or fancied) that he and Marguerite were in love. I thought that Marguerite was terribly sophisticated, sitting there with her drink and her cigarette, from which she blew elaborate smoke rings. They talked, she and the dark young man, about painting, about poetry, about the pronunciation of the word "extraordinary." (Why do I remember that?) Marguerite leaned forward intently. She was rapt, caught up in the presence of the dark young man. She quoted Edna St. Vincent Millay, "Euclid alone has gazed on beauty bare." She quoted again, "Only until this cigarette is ended." (Does she remember quoting Millay? Probably not. A poet who has become unfashionable.) The dark young man quoted W.H. Auden in return. I fell in love a little, I think, with both Marguerite and the dark young man. And more deeply in love than I had been before with painting.

That, of course, was the essence. That was what she left out of her story, because she didn't know it. How could she?

I couldn't sleep that night, I remember. I lay awake in the little room in Mrs. Curtis' house, reconstructing the dimly lit studio, inwardly posing Marguerite and the dark young man. I could have painted them. In fact I sketched them together the next day on the back of an envelope in my purse, as I was going home on the train. Maybe the envelope that contained my cheque, I don't know. I never saw the dark young man again (he is dead now, I think) and I did not see Marguerite for over twenty years.

That is not to say, however, that she disappeared from my life. Far from it. There were in the early years her letters, which came from time to time from different cities, from Montreal, Toronto, Vancouver. She learned to type, and her letters came now typed on yellow paper, but still rapid, exclamatory, decorated with those marginal flying creatures. Marguerite doesn't remember the letters. She thinks I have kept them because of some strange passion for documentation—if indeed I have kept them. She wavers between thinking I keep letters, diaries, documents, old sketches because I am unimaginative and need them to lean on, and that other (disquieting?) possibility that I haven't kept them at all, or that I am inventing letters that perhaps never even existed. It's strange that she isn't able to imagine why I kept them, or why I might invent them if I hadn't received them. She can imagine the phoenix, the unicorn, the marriage of heaven and hell, the day of judgment. She can even imagine my parents, though she hasn't got them quite right. (My father didn't have rough, callused hands, as she thinks. He had beautiful hands of which he was rather proud. It's a detail, but important, as physical details so often are.) In spite of her ability to imagine (and I always told her she was the imaginative one) she can't

95

imagine why I kept her letters. I marvel.

We had lost track of each other for a while when I wrote to her again, that year I was home with a back injury. I had been thrown from a horse, and spent six months or so in a cast recovering back home in Kasoba, with my mother fussing over me. A dull space of time, but I did a lot of work that year. I was beginning to get some reputation by then—I suppose that's why I thought I could write her again. She invited me to visit her in Vancouver if I ever reached there: but by the time I went to Vancouver she was somewhere else, New York I think, and I lost track of her again.

I seemed always to be arriving in places after Marguerite had left. Montreal, Toronto, Vancouver, London, Paris. I spent a year in Boston; she spent a year in New York. We shared a number of the same friends at different times. We won the same awards for different reasons. For a short time, in Vancouver, I even had the same lover as Marguerite had had. Not for long, though. I felt, perhaps unreasonably, that comparisons were being made, and looked elsewhere.

It's hard to say what Marguerite meant to me—the idea of Marguerite, that is to say. A Muse, an ideal? Perhaps. A friend, an older sister, a rival? All of those. A model? Definitely not. Influences work in peculiar ways, as I am tempted to tell the young person who is doing a thesis on my work. One may be influenced to go in the same direction or in the opposite direction. If Marguerite insists on painting the phoenix or the day of judgment, I must paint marigolds or geraniums. Or if I paint the phoenix, I must demonstrate that he flies like a crow, or the day of judgment resembles a farm auction in the Depression. I can't, or won't, paint like Marguerite any more than I would dress like Marguerite or talk like Marguerite. I am inexorably, stubbornly myself. Marguerite doesn't need to be stubborn. It has never occurred to her to be anyone but herself. She never kept my letters and doesn't even remember them, or thinks she doesn't. But where has she got that picture of my parents, inaccurate though it is, except from the letters and sketches I sent her?

Marguerite was out of the country for a number of years, in Athens, in Calcutta, in Rio de Janeiro. Her paintings showed the effects of that restless wandering. During that time I came home, after my parents' deaths, to the prairie, dug myself in, settled down, became that painter whose "deliberate ordinariness elevated to the level of myth" pleased some art critics, though definitely not all. During the last ten years or so, since she came back to Ottawa, I have seen Marguerite a number of times. We have visited each other's exhibitions, admire each other's work as much as sisters ever admire each other's work.

"I always knew we would see each other again," she tells me when I visit her that first time in Ottawa. "People who are important to each other always recur in each other's lives. It's part of the pattern."

I see that she envisages us in a tapestry woven by some great celestial artist. She has made tea for me; we drink it ceremoniously, a communion. I look at her doubtfully over the teacup. She has been important to me, oddly, all these years, but if I have been important to her, I am trying to imagine how.

The Real Truth

I have just finished breakfast and am drinking another cup of tea. It is a dark morning in Ottawa, around 9.10 AM. My window faces the east, and I can see a large ball of light, rather low in the sky, behind mist.

I look around my apartment, a furnished apartment, comfortable and almost anonymous. There is a chesterfield, upholstered in dark green, and two armchairs, one green and one a

98

sort of dark orange. There is a dining-table, from which I have had my breakfast, and four dining-chairs. On the table is a blue jar containing some trailing green plant that a friend has given me, and an orange candle, also a gift, which has not yet been lit. I never think to get matches. In one corner there is a television. There is a coffee-table and there are a couple of end-tables and a lamp with a green base.

Behind my chair is a chest of drawers that acts as a desk and as a room divider. On its top are a typewriter (rented), my transistor radio, an alarm clock, a desk calendar, a box of Kleenex, a dictionary and an atlas and some books of poems, including one or two books I have written myself.

Behind the chest of drawers is my bed, which I have just made, and I can see through to the kitchen, where I must go and wash the dishes.

I came here two weeks ago, at the beginning of January. I am trying to write a novel about someone named Jane who is rather like me but not quite. Jane is a good housekeeper. At least I have said so in the novel. She would probably not have left those dishes unwashed. But now I have washed them.

Now the sun has come out, quite bright, and is almost too dazzling. It shines on the orange—no, it is maroon—chair. I see I have left my slippers in front of the chair. I must move to a corner of the room that is not so bright.

I am having difficulties with the novel. Jane is like me, and yet she isn't like me. How is she unlike me? At the times when she is unlike me, does she fade off and become unreal?

Yesterday I did not do much work. A friend was coming for lunch, Ben Freeman. I find lunch a hard meal to plan for, because when I am by myself I have a sandwich and an apple. But I reheated a beef casserole that is really a stew, like my mother's beef stew, only that I have added mushrooms and green peppers and tomatoes, which my mother would not have put in a stew. I had to run down to the IGA on Elgin Street for vegetables for a green salad.

99

Ben is a pale, lean man, hollow-cheeked, in his early forties. He is a civil servant, but I should not say a dedicated one. He has had a heart condition for a dozen years or so, has had two coronaries, and perhaps a sense of the precariousness of life makes him seem detached from the usual ambitions. At one time we worked together for three years. I thought then that I was in love with him, but now I don't think so any longer. I still like him, however.

Yesterday was bright and sunny, as today is now. We had to draw the curtains to keep the sun off the dining-table. I poured a little sherry into fruit juice glasses. "The dishes come with the apartment," I apologized. "They're rather peculiar."

The stew casserole thing had turned out quite well. I am not a bad cook, though I don't much put my mind to it. Anyhow Ben liked it.

We talked about universities, about the western university in the town where I had lived for the past few years, and from which I am now on leave while I write my novel.

"Do you think students there still have any of the feeling we once had," he asked, "that the university offers a kind of secular salvation?"

I hesitated, considering. "Perhaps you weren't close enough to them to know?" he continued.

"Well," I said, "I taught a creative writing class. They were undergraduates. They weren't student radicals. I shouldn't say they had strong feelings pro or con the university. Then I sat in on a graduate course last term. They were nervous about jobs, of course, but I think they hoped hard times would be over by the time they got their degrees. I shouldn't say they thought of universities as offering salvation, but I think some of them quite liked what they were doing."

"You might not be a good judge," he said. "After all, for you, university has been your salvation. You came from a poor background, and university has given you all you have."

"All I have," I said ironically, looking around the furnished apartment. "And what is that?"

"Quite a lot, I think. Moderately good jobs. Status. A chance to do what you like."

"Oh, a chance to do what I like, yes. That's important. To be honest, I find it hard to imagine what life would have been like for me if I hadn't gone to university. But it might have been possible. There's Alden Nowlan, now. He didn't finish high school, but I think he's read as many books as I have, and maybe he's a better writer. I don't suppose he has much security, but then neither do I. But he works in a university, even if he didn't attend one."

"Still, many people have it in for the universities, and I can't say I blame them. Education was to save the world, and it hasn't."

"Serves people right for expecting one institution to do everything. How many pills do you have to take?" He had lined up a whole assortment, of varying sizes.

"A lot, at noon. I have angina now in addition to the other heart condition."

I wished I had not said anything.

"What is your cottage in the country like?" I ask. "Is it near water?"

"Near a waterfall. It's very pleasant. You must come out some time when the warm weather comes—for several days, if you like."

"That would be nice. Do you still take the long walks you used to?"

"No, I can't do too much. But maybe I will again. I get tired of being careful. I've almost decided that the next time I have pains around my heart I won't stop walking, as I usually do. I'll just go on."

"Do you think you should?" I felt I ought to argue with him about it, but he is stubborn. Would probably run up hill if told not to. Anyhow, I know what he means. What's the use of life if you have to be careful all the time?

Leaving, he said, "Are you busy next week? There's a place you might like for lunch."

"I'll be out of town for a few days. Phone me anyway."

16 January, Sunday

Last night I had dinner with some old friends, a political journalist and his wife. Pete is a big man, nearly 6′5″. He is worried about his health, he has told me on the phone. The doctor has told him to lose 50 pounds. "How much do you weigh?" I ask, mildly curious.

"Two hundred and eighty-five pounds," he tells me.

He does not, when he comes to pick me up in his station-wagon, look especially fat, just big, as he always has.

I have known Pete for twenty years or so. Like me, he is working-class born, depression bred. His father was a railway worker. He himself has worked as a miner, a bar tender, a garbage collector, a school teacher. He was in the Army during the Second War, as a private. He spent a few years as a politician. He is a restless, energetic man, a compulsive worker. When I first knew him, in his early thirties, he attracted me by his gusto for life. I am not sure that his enthusiasm for life is as great now as it was then. Nevertheless, he is still basically an optimist. Now he has decided that he is after all in better health than he thought he was. He has had a bug of some sort and is getting over it, he thinks.

"Your heart is all right?" I ask, thinking of poor Ben, who looks much less of candidate for a heart condition.

"I think so. I'm having some tests for different things that might be wrong. But I'm sure it was just flu. For a few days I almost thought that maybe I should get some kind of quiet job, go off to the bush somewhere."

"Well, why not? Wouldn't that be a good thing? It sounds rather attractive."

"God, no, it sounds like suicide."

Pete and Verna live outside of Ottawa, in a suburban area. Verna comes downstairs in a dressing-gown, yawning. The two younger boys have been playing hockey. The eldest boy is at Toronto, in his first year of university. They seem to me an almost incredibly wholesome family. One of the boys cooks the steaks for dinner. We gather around the table. Pete groans because he is not allowed potatoes.

Pete has just heard that someone, one of his and Verna's old acquaintances, a woman, is to be run as an NDP candidate in a by-election. "They don't think she will win," he says, "but she will make a good candidate."

"I don't know," Verna says, "she may well win. Claudia is very intelligent, very able. I personally think she's dishonest and insincere, but that doesn't mean she isn't competent."

"Why do you think she's dishonest and insincere?" I ask.

"Well, she's just phoney, one of those English middle-class university socialists that the NDP seems to be so full of these days."

"Of course the NDP is middle-class academic," I say, laughing. "Most working-class people are conservative, as we know. But is Claudia more insincere than the average?"

"Tell her about the signs, Verna," Pete says.

"Oh, the signs. Well, you know, the first time Pete ran for office, back in the fifties, of course Claudia and Don, her husband, were helping with things behind the scenes. And the CCF, as it was then, was very poor. We depended for advertising chiefly on those signs people put up on their lawns. Well, the workers were getting people to put up signs and one of them came to Pete and said that Claudia refused to have a sign on her lawn."

"But if they were working with you, why not?"

"I suppose they didn't want to commit themselves, especially Claudia. And she always wanted to be in society and a community leader, and most of the community leader types were Liberals."

"But she will have to put up signs now?"

"Oh, of course," Pete said. "In the last election they left the signs in her basement."

"But," Verna continued, "I don't think her convictions have changed. I don't think she's suffered a conversion or seen the light. Circumstances have changed, not Claudia. She can now be a community leader and belong to the NDP."

"Do you think of running again yourself, ever?" I ask Pete.

"No, I think not. There's nothing I want to do in politics now. Except to get rid of the present prime minister. That I'd like to do. But that's hardly a positive reason for going into politics."

We talk about Ray, the eldest boy. "Is he enjoying Toronto?" I ask.

"He's doing rather well, but I think he might quit," Pete says.

"Do you think he will quit?" I ask Verna.

"Pete and I don't agree on this subject," she tells me.

Later, with Pete and the boys watching television, she talks to me for a while about Ray. Ray is intelligent, he is curious about things, he likes to write; but he is not sure that university matters. He is also unhappily in love. Perhaps it might not harm him to drop university, at least for a few years, but Pete does not like the idea.

"The trouble is," she says, "for Pete university was an exciting experience. He was into everything, sports, societies and so on. He was also good academically. But Ray's a loner; he isn't at all like Pete. And he isn't excited by university."

"Don't you think, Verna," I ask, "that university did something for us that is maybe unnecessary for Ray? At least, I wouldn't for myself have known how to start reading around in a subject. But Ray has been brought up with books and ideas. University can't be as fresh an intellectual experience for him as it was for us. And Pete didn't go to university when he was just out of high school. He went from a battlefield. He had probably had enough real life to be satisfied without more for a few years."

What would Ray, or Ray's girlfriend, think of Jane, the girl in my novel? Would her childhood, her growing up, seem to them incredibly distant, taking place in the years before the flood? The time is so different, even though it is nominally not long ago. And New Brunswick, one has to admit, is still a peculiar little world of its own. Still, I can only try to make it clear. I happen to believe in the value and interest of history, and every human being is a part of history.

Monday, 17 January

This morning when I drew the curtains I could see that snow was thick on the ground and that it was still falling. It looked like mild, soft snow, so I knew that the weather must have moderated in the night.

Yesterday was cold, around sixteen below, with a wind blowing. It felt almost like prairie weather. I decided to go to a Quaker meeting out on Fourth Avenue, and bundled up in a heavy coat and wool scarf. I caught a bus on Bank Street, with not many people on it. The meeting-house was a small church that had been remodelled. I was a few minutes late arriving, and people were already sitting in a silent rectangle in chairs around the room. As in all Quaker meetings, the room had no front, no altar or pulpit on which to focus attention. There was a plain table in the centre of the room with a few books on it. The floor was carpeted in red, and there were white curtains at the windows. Through the curtains a tree was visible, bare of leaves.

I found a chair and sat with my eyes closed for a while. I am not sure whether I am a religious person or not, but the silent meeting fulfils some need. Then I opened my eyes and looked curiously around the room. Perhaps 30 people of varying ages, dressed mostly with a somewhat elaborate casualness. I would judge a number of academics. I remember a friend's self-criticism of Quakers, that they tend to be middle-class liberals, almost always intentionally shabby but rarely necessarily so. I also remember Verna's comments of the night before about the NDP. The same sort of people?

What about Jane? Would she vote NDP and attend Quaker meetings? I somehow see her as perhaps becoming high Anglican and disliking politics. She would perhaps vote Liberal, if she bothered to vote. But Jane has a habit of becoming me, so perhaps she might now and then go to a Quaker meeting.

Pete had said, the night before, that the churches had all crumbled, that religion was finished, at least in our time. What about the people here this morning? These were not all older people, clinging to the emotional security of the past. Many of them were young. But Pete would probably say that this was not what he meant by religion. He meant a formal institution with definite dogmas, a settled liturgy and a relatively unchanging ethical code, something like the Roman Catholic Church before Pope John, or the Presbyterian Church before it became part of the United Church of Canada.

A man got up and started to talk, something about communication without words. He got somewhat tangled up in the words with which he was now trying to communicate. I understood what he meant. Yes. But I am a verbal person. Clumsy as language is.

I thought of Ben. I thought of him going on walking with a pain around his heart. Why hadn't I argued with him? I should telephone him and tell him to take care of himself. Mind your own business, Clara. That's what you would say—in your own mind—if someone said that to you.

After the meeting there was coffee. I talked to a man who told me he came from New Brunswick. It turns out he graduated from Milton High School, which is where Jane studied. (I almost said so, but who is Jane?) "I went to Milton this summer," I told him. "I used to have relatives living there."

"I was there at Thanksgiving," he said. "I liked it better when it was smaller. They've built a lot on to the school."

"It still seems small to me," I told him.

He showed me around the Meeting House, the library and the children's room and the young people's lounge.

"I've just been a Friend for ten years," he told me.

I almost asked him what church he used to attend in Milton, but decided not to. The same one as Jane attended? Probably not.

"Did you know Moss Lake too?" I asked him.

"Visited it once," he said. "I don't remember it very well."

This morning I had a phone call from Stephanie Hyde, suggesting lunch. Stephanie works in the Library of Parliament and I was to meet her there shortly before one. I walked over to the Hill through a light, rather pleasant snow. We had lunch in the cafeteria in the West Block.

"What are you doing in Ottawa?" Stephanie asks over our sandwiches.

"Writing a novel about New Brunswick."

"That sounds logical. You're in Ottawa to write a novel about New Brunswick."

"Well, I'm revising it. It's been written once."

We talk about Winnipeg, where Stephanie grew up and where I used to work. Also about Kingston, which I plan to visit.

"How is the job?" I ask.

"Dull," she tells me. "It was interesting to begin with, when there was more trouble, but now everything's going smoothly."

"You should go around smoothing people's troubles. Move from spot to spot."

"Sometimes I think of the West Coast. Somewhere to retire to."

"Could you stand all that rain?" I ask. "A prairie girl like you?"

It's not likely she will move, really. She has just bought a house, a townhouse, she tells me. "I think I'm growing like my father as I get older," she says. "All the time I was growing up we lived in rented houses because he thought he might move from Winnipeg, though he never did. Then when he was nearly ready to retire he bought a house."

"We all grow to be like our parents," I say. "I know I do."

And Jane. I suppose Jane must grow to be like her parents.

Friday, 21 January

I am back from my trip to Kingston. I went over yesterday morning by bus, through dark, cloudy weather. Shortly before I arrived snow began to fall, and it fell most of the afternoon in thick, soft flakes. I was staying with a young couple, a history professor and his wife, with two small children. The wife also writes poetry. I was doing a poetry reading in the evening at the Art Gallery. It went off well enough, I think.

This is the town where Jane's sister Vickie lived for a time during the last War. I walked around trying to decide where she might have lived. Albert Street? Alfred Street? I lived here myself twenty years ago. This is where I met Pete and Verna. Ray was born that year. He was a healthy, sturdy, good-looking baby. I rather envied Verna, I remember. I used to see a lot of them that year. They suspected, I think (rightly, as it happened) that I did not always have enough to eat, and used to ask me in to share their spaghetti and meatballs. They had not much money either, but Verna was a good manager. Verna was the same age as I, Pete a few years older. In a way I think they saved my life—maybe literally.

Today, after the snow and in sunny weather, the town seemed to sparkle. A handsome old town, not too much modernized yet, I see.

A letter from Adrian in the mail when I got back to Ottawa. I stood reading it in the hall, unbuttoning my coat, smiling as I thought of Adrian, balancing Adrian against Ben in my mind.

Saturday, 22 January

I was out again to see Verna and Pete. They were curious about my trip to Kingston, how I had found the place. Verna wants me to have a talk with Ray while I am in Toronto, where I'm going to see my publisher. He is taking a course in Canadian poetry, and would be interested in talking to someone who writes. Also, I think she wants to find out how he is, whether he is unhappy. She will phone him up, she says, and ask him to phone my hotel.

I asked Pete to drive me home early, as I am taking a morning bus to Toronto. He talked about his sons on the way, with a mixture of pride and anxiety. "Ray is the only one I really worry about," he said. "He wants too much to be liked, and he finds it hard to make friends. For the others it's easy. And he's like Verna, he gets depressed easily."

"Is Verna easily depressed?" I asked. "She usually seems cheerful to me, but I suppose I see her from the outside. I'm happier myself than I used to be."

"Perhaps we all are. Past our stormy twenties and thirties."

Sunday, 23 January

The bus for Toronto left at ten. A dull trip, with a crying baby behind me. I read a novel. Not a bad novel, but sometimes the novel form as such bothers me. It formalizes life too much, excludes what seem to the author irrelevant facts, builds up to artificial climaxes. How do you know what facts are going to turn out to be, improbably, relevant? (I said to Verna last night, when we were talking about the popular vocabulary of the time, that the word I most disliked was "relevant." She thought maybe "swinging." Pete thought "love.") Life, I can't help thinking, is often irrelevant, illogical, episodic, anti-climactic. It is full of false starts. People you suppose may be important to you turn out not to be, and major characters steal onto the stage without your noticing. Sometimes steal off that way, too.

We stopped midway on the trip for lunch. I bought a cheese sandwich and an apple and ate lunch on the bus.

It was after three when we reached Toronto. My hotel-room looks out on a wall, but is comfortable enough.

I lay down for a while to rest, and while I was lying with my eyes closed the telephone rang. It was Ray, wanting to know when he could see me. I suggested that I would have a very early dinner and meet him afterwards in the hotel for a cup of coffee.

Around 7.30 he phoned up to my room. "I'll meet you by the elevators, wearing a red dress so you'll recognize me," I said.

"I'll recognize you all right," he told me.

Of course he has seen me often while he has been growing up. Probably I haven't changed as much as he has. A good-looking boy, rather like Verna. We talk over coffee for a couple of hours. "I like poetry, but I don't know what to say about it," he tells me.

I gather that he is living in a rooming-house, not in residence. "Do you have friends in your classes?" I ask.

"Not really. Just acquaintances. I was friendly with another boy where I live, but he left. He had an argument with the landlady." He smiles, recalling the argument.

"Sometimes it doesn't seem real," he says. "We go to classes and all those people come from real worlds to talk to us, and they are real, but we aren't real, and the classes aren't. It's all interesting, but I don't think it's—relevant."

He brings out the word with a note of discovery, as if it weren't a cliché. I don't smile. I don't even want to. I know the experience he's talking about, and the word doesn't much matter. Don't I remember saying something of the sort to a roommate once in graduate school? I was more unkind than he was, though—I doubted the reality of my teachers as well as the reality of my classmates. Sometimes I doubted my own reality. Sometimes still do.

I'm interested that he misses his family. I had thought perhaps young people now would not admit to being homesick. "The others say it's so nice to be away from home and free," he tells me, stirring his coffee. "I don't see what's so good about it."

I missed home when I went away, I remember. Jane missed Moss Lake. But then there was the difficulty of coming back.

I wish very much that I could help him. He looks so vulnerable. I think of all the years in which a human being can be miserable, and how little anyone can help anyone else.

Still, he enjoys talking about poetry. He has brought along the anthology he is studying, and he opens it at some poems he has marked with a slip of paper.

Partly, I decide, it's just that young people look more vulnerable, because they have not yet been hurt often enough to acquire an effective mask. The middle-aged can also be wounded, but we are old veterans, and can sometimes camouflage our scars. Well—I am amused at "relevant" as a fad word. But I remember a time when "camouflage" seemed to me a modish word too. When I was younger than Ray; when Jane was younger than Ray.

After he has gone I go up to my room in the elevator. I realize that I am holding a piece of paper in my hand, the paper with which he had marked his place in the anthology. I see that it is a piece torn out of some sort of church bulletin with a phone number scribbled on it. Religion, I remembered Pete saying, is finished in our time. How little parents know about their children. How little any one of us knows about each other.

Tuesday, January 25

Last night to dinner with the Winterbournes, whom I had known in the west. They are both writers, both in their early thirties. They have lately bought a house, but have not yet bought much furniture (lack of time or money?) so that we sit around on cushions. I feel a momentary regret that Ray has not met them instead of me, if he wanted to meet writers. They might be more what he would have thought writers should be like. Jane, I decide, would have thought Anne Winterbourne brilliant and enigmatic and would have envied her terribly. I envy her a little now myself, but only a little. I also notice that she is tired, and I feel for her something of the pity I felt for Ray. She drives herself too hard. She is ambitious, as Jane was. Some tension between her and her husband, perhaps?

There are several other guests. I am embarrassed momentarily because I am wearing a dress and the other women are wearing slacks. When I was younger I was often underdressed and now sometimes I find myself overdressed. I decide that it doesn't matter. Jane worried too much about clothes. Why should I?

We talk at dinner about Women's Lib. Anne says she has gone to meetings of a women's group, but that they have spent too much time talking about whether they should wear false eyelashes. "I told them finally," she says, "that I couldn't waste any more time talking about non-essentials. I have my living to earn."

Actresses, somebody says, are badly treated. Speaking of false eyelashes.

But then, somebody else says, so are actors.

There is an argument about why anyone should want to act anyway. One of the other guests, who writes plays, thinks all actors are stupid. I remember having wanted to be an actress when I was young. "I thought I didn't have any personality," I explain. "But if I acted I could invent a personality for myself. I think maybe I write for the same reason."

It crosses my mind that I might have made Jane an actress. Not an illogical ambition for her. Too much to find out about actresses, I decide. Another time, maybe.

I am rather tired after my visit to Toronto. Seeing people in the publisher's office. We talked about my new book of poems, which is due out in the spring; about the revision of the novel. Now I am trying to tidy things up, to write letters.

I think about Jane. Why does she sometimes not seem real? Is it because she is too much like me, and I am not real? Is it because I've left out or diminished some really essential part of me? My desire to write? But I don't like novels about novelists. Or is this a novel?

I see Ray as being rather like Jane. He is alone; he is afraid of his aloneness. He is puzzled by the world, by a sense of unreality, of life rushing away. But the world he is afraid of is not quite the same as the one she was afraid of. It is converging on him more rapidly, tightening in. Or do I just think that now? It's just in retrospect that events seem to move in slow motion. The War was slow, though. But then so is the Vietnam War.

I should phone Ben. He has never phoned me after all—perhaps when I was out of town.

Better not. He doesn't like people breathing down his neck. And anyway I am weighing him against Adrian. Adrian is cleverer than Ben, wittier, better looking. But older, much older than I am.

I don't matter at all to either of them, I think. But let's not be bitter.

Monday, 31 January

Ben is dead. This is the difference between life and a novel, that in a novel his death would have been prepared for. Well, after all, it was prepared for.

Last night I was sitting writing about Jane—Jane in high

school. The phone rang. I was in the middle of a sentence. It was George Foley, who had been friendly with Ben and me before Ben had his first heart attack, though he's quite a bit younger than both of us. Now he lives in Montreal.

"Why, George," I said, pleased. "Are you in Ottawa? Were you here for the weekend?"

"No—I'm here—in Montreal. What I wanted to ask you was, have you seen Ben lately?"

"Ben—why, fairly lately. A week or so ago."

"You haven't seen him since Friday?"

"No. I was out of town. I haven't been in touch. Is he not well again?"

"I think he's dead." He spoke the word as if he were apologizing to me for something.

"Dead? Oh, no."

"I'm sorry to break the news this way. Look, I'm not sure. We heard—somebody said he had died on Friday, but I couldn't find out for sure. I thought you might know. I got your number from Information."

"I don't know. I could phone him up, and if he answers then it's all right. But if he's dead I mightn't be able to find out until tomorrow morning. Then I can phone his office."

"Well, let me know if you find anything out."

After putting the phone down I stood for a minute, considering. Then I dialled the number of Ben's house in the country. He had written the number on a scrap of paper, which I held in my hands. I did not expect an answer. The phone rang twice and then a feminine voice said "Hello?"

"Is Ben there?" I asked, uncertainly.

"I'm afraid not," the voice answered, also uncertainly.

"Is he dead? I heard he was dead."

"Yes, he died Friday. I'm his niece, from Calgary."

"Oh. I've met your mother," I said. "She isn't there?"

"No, I'm afraid she's not here." The voice, which is young, is near to tears.

"Well, perhaps you might tell her," I say. "It's Clara Flagg.

She'll probably remember me."

"Oh." The voice must know my name. "There's a memorial service Tuesday morning." She mentions the undertaker's name, and I write it down, with the time of the service. I realize that I have written it on top of Ben's scribbled note.

I know I should say something appropriate and consoling to the niece. "I'm very sorry," I say. "it's a great shock."

Perhaps more to me than to her, when I think of it.

I phoned George again and told him the news was true.

"I was very fond of Ben," I said.

"I know you were. So was I. But he had his life. He lived it the way he wanted to. By himself. There was no arguing with him."

I undressed for bed, but did not lie down for a time. I sat in the maroon chair and thought of Ben. It was like him to go away so suddenly, without saying anything and with no forwarding address. Tears were running down my cheeks, and I let them run, knowing he disliked tears. Damn Ben, anyway. No, I didn't mean that. But did he intend it? Why hadn't I telephoned him?

This morning I got up late. It was a sunny morning. I wandered out aimlessly, looking in shop windows. My eye was caught by a sale sign in one of those shops that sells expensive china and crystal. I bought four wine glasses, thin and transparent. "These are good crystal," the saleswoman said as she wrapped them up. "The very best. No flaws in them. They're just on sale because the line has been discontinued."

Tuesday, 1 February

I got up at seven, while it was still dark, had breakfast as usual, dressed, did the dishes. I think I had some notion I was going out to meet Ben.

The memorial service was at ten o'clock. I took a bus, was among the first people to arrive. Took a seat near the rear of the chapel. Gradually the chapel filled up. All the people were strangers except his sister, who came in just before the service started, with some other relatives, from a side door. No coffin in view. No flowers. A florid sermon by a minister who spoke of sunsets and afterglows. Two psalms read. The whole thing took half an hour. The conclusion of a life. It's not fair, I think.

I came back on the bus, was carried past my stop and had to walk back. No mail for me at home. I wrote to George to tell him about the funeral. "I want flowers when I die," I said.

The most difficult thing to accept about life is death.

For the past dozen years Ben has known every day that it might possibly be his last day. What does that consciousness do to a man?

He thought it gave him a special dispassionate insight. I'm not so sure. Maybe to accomplish much in life one needs the sense that it will go on a long time. Otherwise what is the point of starting a novel? Or a family?

Wednesday, 2 February

Was talking to Ben's sister on the phone.

In the afternoon Lin Jardine came to see me. We are both in Dorothy's new anthology. She had phoned on Monday; but I suggested she wait for a day or so before dropping in. I couldn't quite face a new person so soon after Ben's funeral.

She is having trouble with a friend who depends too heavily on her for emotional help. She thinks of withdrawing, but feels guilty about the withdrawal. The friend is being psychoanalyzed, and the friend's husband is also being psychoanalyzed in order to be able to understand his wife. Now, Lin says she almost feels she also needs therapy. Perhaps then her husband would need it. The situation is probably in fact painful, but somehow sounds comic. Lin recognizes this fact and laughs. She is a small dark girl with short straight hair and bangs and an easily amused face. I decide that I like her.

Thursday, 3 February

A snowy day, almost a blizzard.

What a weary job to rewrite something. Like unravelling a knitted scarf and knitting it over again. The wool tangles more easily than when it is fresh.

Ben told me once that I was not willing enough to look hard at painful things. I must not omit the painful and ugly aspects of Jane's life. The way in which events distort her personality.

Poor Ben. He had no children and no books. I could at least try to write a book he might have approved of.

And let me not sentimentalize Ben either, just because he's dead. We quarrelled violently enough at one time in the past, before we became more indifferent and peaceable.

Saturday, 5 February

Yesterday there really was a blizzard. Schools and many offices were closed down. When I tried to go for a walk, I saw stuck, abandoned cars. Pedestrians had left the sidewalk and plodded along the street in single file through the thickly falling snow.

Today is fine, bright and cold. People are out shovelling, clearing streets and sidewalks. When I look out my window I can see three or four children, dressed in snowsuits, clustered on a high bank of white snow.

Ben's sister and her daughter were to have flown back to Calgary today. As the storm is over, they have probably gone. I imagine them in an airplane looking down over the white prairie, thinking of Ben. Then they will be back in Calgary;

life will go on as usual; they will miss Ben's letters and phone calls for a while, and then they will gradually forget about him. As I shall forget about him, much of the time.

Wednesday, 9 February

Last night I had a small dinner party. The Edingtons, old friends of mine, the people who gave me my orange candle when I move in, and a young couple, the Vernons, who moved to Ottawa from the west last summer.

Jack and Harriet Vernon arrived first. Harriet is short, rather pretty, with blue eyes and straw-blond hair. Jack is also short, stocky, muscular. He is a former farm boy, and is always conscious of his origins, with a mixture of aggressiveness and apology.

Rather to my surprise, they admired my apartment. "You see what a nice place we could have if only we were free and didn't have kids," Harriet said to Jack.

They have two young children, both almost infants, and Harriet is rather weighed down by them.

After the Edingtons arrived, we went on talking for some time about homesickness. Jack dislikes Ottawa very much. It gives him claustrophobia. He misses the western sky, the sense of space on the prairies. Harriet, on the other hand, thinks she might like Ottawa if she were a little less busy.

We talked about the present hard times. Although he now has a job with the civil service, last year Jack was unemployed and Harriet had to support the family by teaching. This experience has left Jack with a feeling of uncertainty about his capabilities. To my surprise, he thinks some of his difficulties were caused by his education in a country school.

"Do you really think it's a disadvantage?" I asked. "I went to a country school—a one-room country school, at that—and I thought it was an advantage. One's teachers didn't interfere with one's education."

"Oh, perhaps that's true, academically. It's politically and socially that there was a disadvantage. It was always the people who had been to the big city high schools who managed things, who were politically and socially active. In a career, that sort of activity counts more than academic ability. If you want to acquire power."

"That matters to you, then? Being politically and socially active? Acquiring power?"

I wonder if what he says is true. Pete is almost the only politician I know very well, but he went to a small-town school and attended university late. But then he has no lack of self-confidence. If he had wanted to acquire power, I think perhaps he could have done so rather easily. For some reason he seems to have stopped wanting to acquire it, if he ever did. He always enjoyed the ability to exasperate the powerful more, I think.

Dick Edington mentioned a poetry reading Friday night at Carleton. Harriet and I have agreed to go together.

This morning I had a letter from the Distress Centre, thanking me for a cheque I had sent in memory of Ben. I gather Ben had done quite a lot of work for it. For people considering suicide.

Saturday, 12 February

Last night Harriet and I went to the poetry reading at Carleton. Harriet called for me in her car. As neither of us has much sense of direction, we both were muddled finding our way around the campus and through the tunnels.

"Do you often have dreams of being lost in large public buildings?" I asked Harriet, as we were finding our way back to the car park after the reading. "I'm sure I'll have one tonight."

"No, I don't have vivid dreams. I'm always envying Jack because he has these vivid dreams in technicolour. He didn't even realize that he was favoured, that most people dream in black and white, until I told him."

"My nightmares are always in colour. I'm not sure about my pleasanter dreams—I think they're rather pastel."

I should notice my dreams more. I wonder what dreams Jane had, waking and sleeping.

I couldn't remember last night's dreams, after all.

Have finished reading the book of Carrington's letters. She was Lytton Strachey's great friend, and killed herself after he died.

I remember a time when I was younger, when the death of one person might have made me feel that life was not worthwhile; but I no longer feel so intensely. Have I acquired an admirable independence, or am I just colder? I have not for a long time allowed any one person to matter dreadfully to me. So although I've been saddened by Ben's death I can still enjoy having other people in to dinner.

Perhaps also I have a stronger belief in immortality than I think I have, and I feel Ben is still alive. And, after all, I can't myself expect to have more than twenty or 30 more years of life—not much more, anyway. Perhaps much less. So I ought not to make a fuss.

Sunday, 13 February

Muddled dreams about being in a hotel, trying to reach one particular level in an elevator. The elevator would never work for that floor, only for those above and below it, and I could not find the stairway.

Then a dream of a large banquet in a hotel, but I found the food indigestible. Rather nightmarish dreams, so that I woke up tired and bad-tempered.

Out to Quaker meeting. The Edingtons there. A small crowd.

It was the first time I had been to Meeting since Ben's death, and I sat trying to think of its significance for me. "The bell tolls for me."

I think of Ben, and I think perhaps he was right when he used to argue with me that I cared too much about acquiring fame. Ben didn't care about either fame or money, and I cared hugely about both, though I've given up caring about money. I wanted to be loved, too, as Jane did, and Ben believed in non-attachment. Well, eventually one must detach oneself from all people, possessions, achievements. And yet these ought to matter, within reason, I can't help feeling. Ben carried detachment too far. Or did he? Not for him, presumably. For me.

Should one write a novel to show the unimportance of writing a novel?

Tuesday, 15 February

Lin had invited me to come last night to a poetry class that she teaches and read some of my poems and answer questions. It was a small class, perhaps a dozen students, and I enjoyed meeting them, except that one girl took a dislike either to me or to my poetry (perhaps to both) and did some minor heckling. I was rather surprised by the hostility. She looked a gentle enough girl. I think my impulse when I was younger would have been to say something biting and shut her up for the evening or send her out of the room in tears; but I find myself kinder than I used to be. At first I tried to ignore the dislike, but eventually was obliged to face it. One of the students asked me if I had been friendly with other writers and if they had influenced me. I mentioned a few friends, older people who had been encouraging to me when I was young or younger people whom I found sympathetic. P.K. Page. Dorothy Livesay. Margaret Atwood.

"Did you know Shakespeare too?" the girl asks, in a voice heavy with sarcasm.

I can't, of course, ignore her. "I wish I had," I say to her. She is sitting near me, and I decide that I must speak just to her. "I sometimes feel as if I knew him. I was brought up in a country school with almost no books, nothing but Shakespeare and the Bible and one or two others. And when I grew up and first met a few writers and they were friendly to me, I was thrilled in a way you people wouldn't be, because you probably take books and writers for granted. I guess I was a very naïve young person. Maybe I'm still rather naïve."

I keep my eyes on her face. I want her to realize that I am human and vulnerable, as she is. I think I have made her realize. She drops her eyes.

Later, when I read another poem, she looks up and says, "I like that poem. It's very good." She really does like it, too. I can tell. It's not just that she's suffering from remorse, though of course she is.

Afterwards Lin came home with me for a cup of tea. We had a long rambling conversation, about death and poetry and fortune-telling and our friends. She is worried about Diana, the friend who is being psychoanalyzed. She is frightened of her extreme dependence, also of the fact that Diana manipulates people, that she tells different stories to Lin, to her own husband, to Lin's husband, presumably to her psychoanalyst. She sometimes threatens suicide. She suffers from amnesia.

"But if you meet Diana you will probably hear another version of the story," she says.

"I think I'll avoid meeting Diana," I say. "I'm already writing one novel. If I weren't, I might want to meet her. But you should write it."

"Oh, I leave the novel to her."

"Well, the four of you should write it. From four points of view. With the psychoanalyst doing a fifth part, as God."

She tells me that a friend of hers has lately recovered from an almost fatal illness. "It's like a resurrection. I had given him up and now he's alive again."

She asks me, "Do you run into things like that? Resurrections? Miracles, almost?"

I think of Ben. "Do you believe in resurrection really?" I ask. "Resurrection of the people who are really dead, not just the dying?"

I tell her about Ben. And about my old professor, who died at the beginning of the year. His wife wrote me that she felt his spirit still in the room. I tell Lin now that I can't believe Ben is dead.

"The world is strange," she says. "I feel anything is possible. I think myself that when Christ rose again something really happened; so many people witnessed something. I don't see why Ben shouldn't be here now."

I have a sense for a moment of an outside presence in the room, of Ben, aloof and angular, standing in the doorway in a dark overcoat. Perhaps because two of us have spoken his name.

Because his spirit is in the room, I tell Lin, "We used to argue. He thought I made too much of accomplishment. He thought—and I'm beginning to think he was right—that it mattered more that you should be a certain kind of person than that you should accomplish things."

"I agree with him, I guess," she says. "Ambition bothers me at times, even the desire to do good actions. I feel if I could be still and be myself and not bother to pile up words or acts, perhaps that's what I need to do. I think I might give up writing everything but letters and diaries."

"You keep a diary too? I've kept one for years."

"I keep two diaries. One for day and one for night."

"Why two?"

"The second is for my dreams."

I am delighted with this idea. A diary just for dreams. Unfortunately I can't remember last night's dreams.

Of course, I think this morning, I could no more help writing than a truly confirmed alcoholic can help drinking. Even with the help of an Authors Anonymous. Certainly my writing was more important to me than Ben was. Maybe than Adrian is.

It's not precisely a matter of wanting fame, either. Ben was unjust to me there. It was more that I wanted to make something, to do a good piece of work. All the better if someone else noticed that it was good; but even if they didn't notice, even if it wasn't a good piece of work, at least I wanted to have tried.

Lin has telephoned and said that a local television program wants to interview us on Friday morning. Herself, me, Diana, if Diana is well enough. I don't look forward to the occasion.

Wednesday, 16 February

After several wet, slushy days, today was cool and sunny. I went down to Sparks Street this morning to look for a new blouse to wear with the skirt I thought of wearing on Friday. I looked at one that would have been suitable, but bought another that won't go well with the skirt at all. I can wear it with my old slacks.

In the fitting-room I looked at myself with something like dismay. Without a full-length mirror or bathroom scales, I must be letting myself gain weight. I look blowsy and dowdy, in a shabby skirt that's too tight for me. And I'm half expecting Adrian next week.

Thursday, 17 February

Dream of sitting on a bench with a fair, rather pink-skinned young man whom I had never seen. Although I didn't know him, he was making love to me. I think we were on a university campus, but I'm not sure what campus.

Another dream of talking to two men who were engaged in some kind of business, something to do with trucking. They came from Kingston. One of them told me that he was Diana's brother, and that the other man was his brother-in-law, Diana's husband. I thought that Diana must be the daughter of my old landlady in Kingston. I mentioned an old war movie that I had seen in Kingston, I think a rerun of *All Quiet on the Western Front,* which had horrified me. One of the men said that he had enjoyed it very much. "You learned a lot from it," he said. I wondered if I had been mistaken about the movie. Perhaps I had liked it better than I thought I had.

Now I remember seeing that movie at a film society in Kingston twenty years ago. I had told Pete about it. "How can anyone stand real war when I have to close my eyes just for a movie?" I asked him.

"Reality is never as bad as the movies," he said. "And the second war wasn't as bad as the first, with that old trench warfare and the mud. I guess I enjoyed the war. You made closer friendships than at other times. There was a sense of purpose. How much purpose do we have in life now?"

This morning I had my hair done and had a manicure. I can't be slender and young, but at least I can make an effort.

One of those days in which things go wrong. A button came off my coat and I had to stop to sew it on. The sink in the bathroom was clogged temporarily.

I'm tired of Jane, dull, priggish little girl that she is. But don't dull, priggish little girls have a right to have their lives written? She's just as real as Vickie, the lively sister, isn't she? There are as many people like her?

Friday, 18 February

As I expected, I disliked seeing myself on television. I look a pleasant enough, conventional middle-aged woman, as I suppose I am; but of course one never sees oneself as that. One doesn't realize how instinctively one protects oneself, so that the shy, absurd, agonized young girl who is still there can't be seen. Not that I want her to be seen; but I don't like the replacement either.

Verna telephoned me in the evening to say she had seen the program. "When I first knew you, you would have hidden from an interviewer," she says.

"We all change, Verna. I ought to have changed more than I have."

"I don't think I've changed. I wish the world didn't keep changing so much, that's all. Living out of town, I don't always realize the difference; and then I go in for a day, or maybe go to a movie, and everything seems different. I don't think it's an improvement, either. Do you?"

"Not particularly. Maybe it isn't as different as it looks, though. A trade-in on surfaces. Our fashions of thinking may be dated, Verna, but you can go on wearing good wool for a long time."

"Yeah. Provided it doesn't shrink."

It's true, Verna's surface has changed less than mine. I think of myself as old-fashioned, but Verna, I suspect, thinks I'm modern. We've known each other so long, and yet we both pretend a little to one another. I can't talk to her, as I have to Pete, about Ben. Or about Adrian—though I've never mentioned Adrian to Pete.

Saturday, 19 February

I've had a painting delivered that I had asked a friend to do. It's of the old house in New Brunswick, near Grand Lake, where I grew up, the house on which I modelled the Marchants' house at Moss Lake. The house is now deserted. The painting was done last September, on a day when the sun was shining through white clouds, yet in spite of the sunshine it is a sad painting. The house is three dimensional and solid, but it is nevertheless ghostly, like a dream or a mirage.

As Jane said of the house at Moss Lake, I loved it more than

126

any person. But I never expect to own it.

I turn off the lights, except for one, and sit in the semi-twilight, staring at the painting. It is as if I were walking up to the house on a dusky evening. Its gables stand out against the pale clouds in the background. The black holes where there were once windows are empty and yet vivid, as if a ghostly light hovered behind them.

Would it not be possible, by an act of will, to bring back the past, so that the windows would be filled once more with glass, and the kerosene lamps lit behind the pane, my mother baking bread in the kitchen? Time, of course, is not real. There would be no time if there were no change.

The painting itself arrests change, and therefore arrests time. But it arrests the wrong time.

Sunday, 20 February

Erase the last chapter of the novel.
    It's impossible.
    Nothing ever happened to Jane.
    What am I implying in that last chapter? That Jane might have married Francis Knight? That at least they might have been lovers?
    Of course this can't be true. I'm only following a convention, or one of two possible conventions: that young girls fall in love and are married, or that they think they are in love and are seduced.
    I know perfectly well that this is not always true. Oh, all young girls think they are in love at some point or another—or they did when Jane was young. But would Francis Knight ever have looked at Jane Marchant? Not likely. It was a daydream.
    Well, he might have looked at her. Why is it so impossible? Okay, he was home from the war, he was lonely, he was on

the rebound from that little bitch Erica.

But what about Jane?

Wouldn't she have refused to go on that drive? You know Jane. You know she wasn't going to take a risk. She was still afraid of Roger Harrigan, that boy who almost raped her.

Well, yes, she was afraid of taking risks, in a way. But time was passing. She was afraid of that, too. Francis Knight was handsome, rich (by her standards), a dominant male. She didn't altogether like him; she thought he was mindless; but she wasn't a sexless girl, though she might try to be. And she had some instincts for social climbing. Anyhow, Francis Knight was not Roger Harrigan. Even a rather stupid girl like Jane knew that. A man with the normal amount of vanity is not a rapist.

But what would a marriage between those two be like? Jane married to Francis Knight? Not so bad as I think, maybe. He was probably brighter than she was. Maybe he would have made her kinder, less of a snob.

I don't know. I honestly don't know.

Anyhow, that last paragraph in the chapter helps, doesn't it? Makes the whole thing ambiguous?

Tuesday, 22 February

Adrian has been here on a brief visit. He telephoned me at noon to say that he would pick me up in the evening to take me to dinner. After all, the weather was so bad that we could not go farther than the Chateau, where Adrian was staying.

I look at him across the table with a certain pride. He is a handsome man, as tall as Pete, with greying fair hair. Jane's Francis Knight would look rather like Adrian by now, I think. He is fond of food and drink, of long elaborate meals, as I am not particularly. Ben in his kitchen, buttering slabs of bread and opening a tin of sardines to go with beer, floats absurdly before me. Ben was not as handsome as Adrian. Not at all handsome, in fact. No, I won't feel guilty about Ben. He didn't love me. I don't think he ever loved me. Adrian doesn't either, but he wants to impress me, and in fact he does, somewhat.

"Is there anywhere you would rather be than here with me?" Adrian asks.

"No. Nowhere." It's the truth, more or less. I've been drinking more than I'm used to. My head seems to float off my shoulders and be stationed somewhere on the other side of the room. Then it comes back to my shoulders again. I look at Adrian's hands, and think how much larger they are than mine. I like hands. They are beautiful objects. Very beautiful. Jane admired hands too, I remember.

After dinner we walk back to my apartment. We can't get a taxi because of the icy streets, and anyway it's not a long walk.

Coffee and the fresh air have made me sober again. We sit together on the chesterfield, and Adrian admires my new painting, my haunted house. We talk of ghosts, of death, and I think once more of Ben. I'd like to tell Adrian about Ben, but I don't know how. "I've had a friend die lately," I say, but I can't seem to say any more.

"We're all vulnerable," Adrian says. "We should be kind to one another."

He puts his hand—which looks like Francis Knight's—on mine, and I think of Jane and how she felt—must have felt—with Francis.

I bury my head in his shoulder, feeling unreasonably guilty toward Ben. They are expert and practised hands. "I'm in good hands," I think, amused by the pun.

I am surprised how badly I want to be in bed with Adrian, how much, when we are, I enjoy the feel of his skin on mine. He is too heavy for me, I feel his weight crush on me painfully, but nevertheless joy flows through me. I ought not to feel this way when Ben is dead. Laughter breaks from my throat when he comes into me, a strange, impersonal laughter, not connected with any amusement.

Later he falls asleep. I am pinned to the bed by his weight, but he wakes up before I feel obliged to wake him.

"Are you all right?" I say, because he looks tired, and I feel a stirring of fright. Maybe he has a heart condition too. Would it have killed Ben, I wonder? But Ben died anyway, just running to catch a bus. Because he was bored with not running. Adrian also is vulnerable, I know. He lost an eye in an accident years ago, still feels himself lacking, I think.

"Don't look so serious," he says. "Is something the matter?"

"No. The light's in my eyes, that's all."

He turns off the light, and puts his arms around me again. "We'll have two minutes' silence," he says. I laugh again, this time in amusement.

Oh, Ben. Poor Ben. Damn Ben, anyway. Why did he die? Why did he have that first stupid heart attack?

Friday, 25 February

Last night Lin came over to see me for a while. We talked of whether it was ever possible to make a change in one's life, to take a decisive step. Or did all one's decisions end up in a life that was very similar to the one already being lived?

"Instead of coming back to Canada from London ten years ago," Lin said, "I might have married a Parsi and lived in Bombay. That would have been a different life."

What about Jane's choice? Did she choose, in the end, to marry Francis Knight? Or did he choose to marry her? I'm not really sure. She did agree to go on that drive into the country.

And if Jane didn't marry Francis Knight? Well, perhaps she went to London and almost married a Parsi from Bombay. Perhaps after all she married Stuart Holmes, who is by this time head of the Department of Political Science in some university or other. Perhaps she is an actress in Stratford. Perhaps she went back to Moss Lake and taught in a rural school—but she would never stay there. All those endings were perfectly possible.

Or perhaps she is sitting in Vancouver or Halifax or Dublin, writing a novel about Moss Lake.

I don't think it matters.

The important thing is that for a while she was really alive. For a while she could love Francis, or think she loved him, beyond all reasons of snobbery or vanity, and that experience would erase Roger Harrigan coming out of the woods and the kids tormenting her in the schoolyard.

Partly erase them, anyway. Nothing is ever quite erased. The other night with Adrian, just for a minute, I thought of Jane and Roger Harrigan. Adrian was holding my throat between his hands—so—and I was suddenly glad I knew so much about him. When you have been raped as a child, you don't want violence again, ever.

But Roger never caught up with Jane.

Or did he?

Saturday, 26 February

I've wasted so much of my life, I think. Jane wasted so much of her life. But how do I know what is waste?

I have no sense of direction. When I'm in a strange city I'm always finding that I've been walking down streets leading the wrong way. I have to turn around, walk back and look at the signposts, ask for directions from pedestrians. But the place I was going to was never as good as the little park where I sat when I was lost, with ducks on a pond. Or the drab eating place that sold fish and chips, very hot and crisp. Or the bookstore where I found the book of poems I hadn't the money to buy, and couldn't find again when I had the money. If I always knew my way I wouldn't have found them.

"I don't drift into things," Ben said to me once. "I choose my way. I'm not like you."

That was before he had his first heart attack. He didn't choose that.

And serve him right for being so purposeful, I think, angry at him again.

How do I know what Jane did with her life after Francis came home. She mightn't have wasted it at all, as I have. If Ben had been Adrian, my life would have been different, I think. (If I had been different, Ben's life might have been different.)

"I wish I had known you when I was young," I said to Adrian the other night.

"But you are young," he answered.

And it's true that when I'm a really old woman I'll remember myself now as young. I have no excuses for dying while I'm alive.

Jane, I think, married Francis Knight, who looks like Adrian, and has a son who is the same age as Ray. No, I can't imagine it. It isn't real.

Adrian is real; and Ben, who is dead, is real; and Jane is real, but she never grew to be any older than 25.

I won't let myself be frightened of life again, I think. Life is full of violence and death and poverty and danger. There's always a war somewhere. Someone could kill you for the money you don't have. You may have a heart attack tomorrow. But life is also full of beautiful, beautiful dullness. And it has its pleasures, like morning with real orange juice. Adrian may not love me, but he will make love to me again. Or, if not Adrian, someone else. I'll write poems for Adrian. For his hands, I think.

For so much of my life, I've said, though maybe not aloud—never aloud—"No, I won't have anything to do with them. They might hurt me." Or, "No, I won't love him; he will die, or move away, or change, or forget me, or laugh at me, and it won't have been worthwhile." Well, I laugh at people myself. I hurt them. I move away and forget them. Some time I'll die. But please God (who may not exist) not yet. Not until I love someone, Adrian or anyone, for a day or a week. I'm not asking for it to last forever. I'm not asking for perfection. Only this temporary touch, this nearness, the attempt to understand.

Jane and Francis could have rebuilt the house, I think. Probably they did, come to think of it.

I look at the painting again. Yes, Jane and Francis rebuilt the house for a summer house. They've planted a garden behind it, and the apple tree behind the house still yields fruit. Somewhere inside the house, Jane, who is after all a good housekeeper, even if I'm not, is putting fresh paper on a wall.

She criticizes Francis—I'm sure she does—because he is not as successful as Stuart, who probably defeated Francis in the last Provincial election. She thinks every now and then that Francis is too commonplace for her, although she is mildly jealous of him with other women. She wants their son to write a novel, though he is not likely to. Nevertheless, as she stands there matching the edges of the wallpaper, I insist that she is singing. She is thinking that she will write the story of her life.

At some time in the future something remarkable is sure to happen.

POSTSCRIPT: *3 February, 1989*

"Which of my hundred truths shall I be true to?" Katherine Mansfield said. And Ian Wedde said, "All writing is fiction of a kind."

I wrote "Clara Flagg's Journal" back in 1972, as a frame for the novel I was writing then, *The Sisters.* Much of the Journal has a strong resemblance to reality. Still, I can see, when I look back on my "real" diary, that there were changes. I concentrated a four-month period into a two-month period. Adrian's visits were more frequent than I've made them. (Of course, his name was not Adrian, and Anne Winterbourne and Lin Jardine have other names, too.) My "real" diary included more notes about letters to publishers, poetry readings, lectures, visits to the bank, ideas for poems, the search for jobs. I was more emotional about Adrian too, I think. I haven't quite told it the way it happened, how it felt. Though not much about feelings is in the "real" diary, either. Maybe I told more in the poems. I don't know if I could re-create the real truth now. Perhaps it would be too sad, now that Adrian is dead. Or would it? I loved Adrian, I loved the way he flattered me, the way he amused me.

I still love Adrian. Ben too. There's no reason now why I can't love both of them.

POEMS FOR YOUR HANDS

I

Your hand, which has written these poems
that I read in the spring evening,
has also traced poems on my flesh.
The inside of my mouth
has flowered into lyrics;
my breasts are rhymed
couplets;
my belly is smoothed to a sonnet;
and the cave of my body
is a found poem.

2

You say you are an old man
un viellard
and I remember you middle-aged when I was young
yet I feel a wistful youthfulness in you
the unquenched spirit
still flaming in spite of time and wrinkles.

Desire is sad
across this gulf of time.

But touch me lightly
touch my tongue with yours.

Perhaps I could not have stood
the total blaze
of your youth and strength.

3

You disarrange my life.
I cannot predict you.
Saying that you do not know me,
I mean that I do not know you.
I know I could not live with you,
but am frightened also
that I may find it hard to live
without you.

4

I try to find out facts
about you, so as to feel safe with you.
I want to know all about your brothers
and what games you played as a child
and whether you were unhappy
and if you are afraid of anything.
All this I shall put together;
I shall make a file on you.

In return, I am willing to let you know
that I am afraid of bridges
and of strangers.

5

Without my glasses on
I cannot see you
am only aware of
arms, legs, a head,
the feel of skin
and hair.

You might be God
or my father
or someone I loved when I was young
who is now dead.

You might be a king
or an astronaut.

You might be an oak.

6

"These are the sort of kisses
Catullus meant," you say.

I wonder if Lesbia ever
wrote any poems.
What a pity
no archaeologist has ever found them.

7

Let us not be
exclusively solemn.
In spite of the theory
that lust is a serious passion,
there is time even in bed
for a little light
verse.

8

"The body knows its mate,"
you say truly
and yet we have our minor difficulties.
But anyhow you tell me
"Next time I'll bring a sign saying
    We shall overcome."

9

You telephone me from your office
where I feel you are bored.

I too have been bored
spring feverish
but I do not say so.

The inconvenience of joy
is that it is habit forming.

10

A pigeon walks along
my window-sill
to prove that spring is here.

I do not need his proof
now that I am able to imagine `
that we are both young again.